Pluggable Authentication Modules

The Definitive Guide to PAM for Linux
SysAdmins and C Developers

A comprehensive and practical guide to PAM
for Linux: how modules work and how to
implement them

Kenneth Geisshirt

BIRMINGHAM - MUMBAI

Pluggable Authentication Modules

The Definitive Guide to PAM for Linux SysAdmins and C Developers

First published: January 2007

Production Reference: 1211206

Published by Packt Publishing Ltd.
32 Lincoln Road
Olton
Birmingham, B27 6PA, UK.

ISBN 978-1-904811-32-9

www.packtpub.com

Cover Image by www.visionwt.com

Credits

Author

Kenneth Geisshirt

Reviewers

Ralf Hildebrandt

Huang Zhen

Development Editor

Louay Fatoohi

Assistant Development Editor

Nikhil Bangera

Technical Editor

Mithil Kulkarni

Editorial Manager

Dipali Chittar

Project Manager

Patricia Weir

Indexer

Bhushan Pangaonkar

Proofreaders

Martin Brooks

Chris Smith

Layouts and Illustrations

Shantanu Zagade

Manjiri Nadkarni

Cover Designer

Shantanu Zagade

About the Author

Kenneth Geisshirt is a chemist by education, and is a strong free software advocate. He spent his Christmas holidays in 1992 installing SLS Linux, and GNU/Linux has been his favorite operating systems ever since.

Currently, he does consultancy work in areas like scientific computing and Linux clusters. He lives in Copenhagen, Denmark with his partner and their two children. You can find him at `http://kenneth.geisshirt.dk/`.

About the Reviewers

Ralf Hildebrandt is an active and well-known figure in the Postfix community, working as a systems engineer for T-Systems, a German telecommunications company.

He speaks about Postfix at industry conferences and hacker conventions and contributes regularly to a number of open source mailing lists. Ralf Hildebrandt is co-author of *The Book of Postfix*.

Huang Zhen is a software engineer at IBM China Development Labs.

He has been working on the Linux-HA project since 2004 and contributed several components to the project.

PAM-related functions in the Linux-HA project were developed by him.

Table of Contents

Preface

PAM (Pluggable Authentication Modules) was introduced in 1996 by two developers at SUN Microsystems, and Solaris 2.6 was the first operating system that used PAM for authentication of users. Today, most UNIX and Linux operating systems implement PAM, and it unifies UNIX across hardware and software. PAM is a modular and flexible authentication management layer that sits between Linux applications and the native underlying authentication system. PAM can be implemented with various applications without having to recompile the application when PAM configuration is changed. This book is a short guide to how PAM works, how it is configured, and how to develop with PAM.

What This Book Covers

Chapter 1 begins with an introduction to the problem of authentication. It outlines the problems of authentication, and discusses how the framework of PAM can provide solutions for the authentication problems and reduce the complexity. This chapter also discusses installing Linux-PAM, and downloading and compiling third-party modules.

Chapter 2 gives you a detailed view on working of PAM, its framework, the PAM file structure, and its architecture diagram. The four management groups (auth, account, session, and password) are introduced and we discuss how they interact with each other using control flags. We then explain the logon process using an example. An example PAM configuration is provided at the end.

Chapter 3 gives the reader methods and guidelines for testing and debugging a PAM configuration. Typical problems in PAM configurations are discussed and a number of simple test cases are analyzed and dissected. We cover the pamtester utility and finally see what not to do when configuring PAM.

Modules are a very central concept in PAM. PAM modules provide the actual services that the application expects. *Chapter 4* is a short guide to modules and the parameters found in most PAM implementations. The usage of modules is explained with suitable examples.

Chapter 5 presents a number of short recipes for using PAM in the real world. This chapter shows how to work with PAM for mounting encrypted home directories, automatic SSH key loading, and directory services like Winbind and LDAP. We also look at a PAM-based alternative to using Apache's htaccess file. We round up the chapter with a discussion on restricting access to r-services and limiting the resources used by users.

The power of PAM lies in its capability to let users extend its functionality by developing new modules. *Chapter 6* introduces us to PAM development and we develop a PAM-aware application. This chapter will also explain how to develop your own custom PAM module in C.

The *Appendix* provides the source code for a PAM-aware application and a PAM module (ssh_tunnels module).

What You Need for This Book

Knowledge of UNIX (or Linux) is required. The reader should not be afraid of command lines. Some knowledge of programming is desirable, in particular of C or related programming languages. No prior knowledge of PAM is required.

Conventions

In this book, you will find a number of styles of text that distinguish between different kinds of information. Here are some examples of these styles, and an explanation of their meaning.

There are three styles for code. Code words in text are shown as follows: "The application initializes the PAM runtime by calling the `pam_start` library function in the PAM library."

A block of code or command-line statements will be set as follows:

```
pamela@pamela:~$ apropos pam
pam (7)                 - Pluggable Authentication Modules
for Linux
pam_authenticate (3)   - authenticate a user
pam_chauthtok (3)      - updating authentication tokens
pam_end (3) [pam_start]  - activating Linux-PAM
pam_fail_delay (3)     - request a delay on failure
pam_get_item (3)       - item manipulation under PAM
pam_getenv (8)         - get environment variables from /
                         etc/environment
```

When we wish to draw your attention to a particular part of a code/command block, the relevant lines or items will be made bold:

```
pamela@pamela:~$ apropos pam
pam (7)                 - Pluggable Authentication Modules
for Linux
pam_authenticate (3)   - authenticate a user
pam_chauthtok (3)      - updating authentication tokens
pam_end (3) [pam_start]  - activating Linux-PAM
pam_fail_delay (3)     - request a delay on failure
pam_get_item (3)       - item manipulation under PAM
pam_getenv (8)         - get environment variables from /
                         etc/environment
```

New terms and **important words** are introduced in a bold-type font.

Reader Feedback

Feedback from our readers is always welcome. Let us know what you think about this book, what you liked or may have disliked. Reader feedback is important for us to develop titles that you really get the most out of.

To send us general feedback, simply drop an email to feedback@ packtpub.com, making sure to mention the book title in the subject of your message.

If there is a book that you need and would like to see us publish, please send us a note in the **SUGGEST A TITLE** form on www.packtpub.com or email suggest@packtpub.com.

If there is a topic that you have expertise in and you are interested in either writing or contributing to a book, see our author guide on www.packtpub.com/authors.

Customer Support

Now that you are the proud owner of a Packt book, we have a number of things to help you to get the most from your purchase.

Downloading the Example Code for the Book

Visit http://www.packtpub.com/support, and select this book from the list of titles to download any example code or extra resources for this book. The files available for download will then be displayed.

The downloadable files contain instructions on how to use them.

Errata

Although we have taken every care to ensure the accuracy of our contents, mistakes do happen. If you find a mistake in one of our books—maybe a mistake in text or code—we would be grateful if you would report this to us. By doing this you can save other readers from frustration, and help to improve subsequent versions of this book. If you find any errata, report them by visiting http://www.packtpub.com/ support, selecting your book, clicking on the **Submit Errata** link, and entering the details of your errata. Once your errata have been verified, your submission will be accepted and the errata added to the list of existing errata. The existing errata can be viewed by selecting your title from http://www.packtpub.com/support.

Questions

You can contact us at questions@packtpub.com if you are having a problem with some aspect of the book, and we will do our best to address it.

1

Introduction to PAM

Welcome to the wonderful world of PAM. PAM is an acronym for Pluggable Authentication Modules. Together with boot loaders PAM lives a quiet life—only a few specialists know and care about their existence.

PAM can do many things for you but the primary focus is to authenticate your users. Moreover, PAM lets you set up the environment the users will work in. And when the users log out, PAM will tear down the working environment in a controlled way.

History of PAM

The history of PAM goes back to 1995 when developers from Sun Microsystems implemented a generic framework for Solaris. When Solaris 2.6 was released in August 1997, PAM was an integrated component of the operating system. Ever since then, Solaris has been using PAM for authentication. In February 1997, the Linux-PAM project began, and most GNU/Linux distributions today are using PAM.

The official website of Linux PAM is `http://www.kernel.org/pub/linux/libs/pam/`, while SUN Microsystems documents the Solaris PAM at `http://www.sun.com/software/solaris/pam/`, and OpenPAM used by FreeBSD can be found at `http://trac.des.no/openpam/`. PAM implementations are based on an open standard from the Open Group named XSSO, which can be found at `http://www.opengroup.org/pubs/catalog/p702.htm`.

The primary operating system of this book is GNU/Linux, but PAM does exist for many operating systems. Configuration files are almost identical across Linux and UNIX operating systems—module names might differ slightly and some modules are not supported on every contemporary UNIX. This means that the examples in this book can be carried from one UNIX environment to another with minor adjustment.

The examples in the book have been tested under Ubuntu Linux 6.06 LTS or SuSE Linux Enterprise Server 9 SP2 (as VMware guests).

PAM Solves the Authentication Problem

Before you can begin working with your computer, you have to log in. At least, this is true in the UNIX world and corporate Windows world. In order to gain access to the computer, the installed software, and data, you have to prove who you are. This is the authentication problem (or solution, depending on your view). Typically, you have to provide two items: a user name and a password. Only if the user name exists in the user database and the password matches, will you gain or be granted access.

Traditionally, UNIX authentication is done by comparing the (encrypted) password for the user in the password file (/etc/shadow for most modern UNIX and Linux systems, and /etc/passwd in the old days), but each program that requires authentication implements its own authentication mechanisms. The wilderness of authentication mechanisms becomes more visible when you add various applications that are doing some sort of authentication. Logging in directly to a graphical user interface requires a display manager, which must be able to validate the users. Now add services like FTP, TELNET, IMAP, SSH, and possibly a growing set of web applications, which require authentication of their users. As a system administrator you will end up spending a lot of time maintaining many user databases besides /etc/passwd. Your might have a nightmare if the user databases become inconsistent, for example, a misspelled user name in one place can be difficult to find. Moreover, the users have to remember many user names and passwords.

Need for PAM

PAM and PAM-aware applications reduce the complexity of authentication. With PAM, the system administrator can use the same user database for every login process of your system—if he or she wishes to do so. Moreover, it is possible to use more than one underlying authentication mechanisms (or back end)—controlled by PAM and transparent to the users. The good news for the systems administrator is that knowledge in one UNIX operating system (one particular PAM implementation) can easily be carried over on to another UNIX operating system. Learning PAM will make you a better UNIX systems administrator.

PAM has a well defined API, and PAM-aware applications will not break if the system administrator changes the underlying authentication configuration.

Furthermore, the password file does not scale. It might work with 100 users, but working with 5000 users is a completely different story. PAM can easily scale to tens of thousands depending on the chosen back end; changing the back end user database, for example, from a flat file to an LDAP server will be painful if you are not using PAM.

Application programmers can take advantage of PAM if an application requires some kind of authentication. Using PAM for authentication requires much less programming than developing a complete set of authentication functions, and the application programmer can rely on the system administrator to choose an appropriate back end to store user names and passwords.

Installing Linux-PAM

In general, the Linux distributions, the BSD family, and Solaris come with a PAM implementation bundled with the operating system as part of the operating environment. In these cases, installation is done as you install the operating system. Slackware is one of the last PAM-free Linux distributions and in UNIX operating systems like AIX, PAM is an add-on product.

In this section, the installation of Linux PAM on Slackware 11 is explained. Installing PAM can be dangerous since you can leave your computer in a state where you cannot log in and correct mistakes.

Downloading

Linux PAM can be downloaded from its website hosted by `kernel.org`. Currently the 0.99.6.3 version of Linux PAM is used. The following commands download and unpack Linux PAM:

```
# wget http://www.kernel.org/pub/linux/libs/pam/pre/
library/Linux-PAM-0.99.6.3.tar.gz
# tar xzf Linux-PAM-0.99.6.3.tar.gz
```

The source code is now located in a directory called `Linux-PAM-0.99.6.3`. But if you are going use PAM, you will need to have PAM-aware applications. The Linux utility (the name of the package is `linux-utils`) contains a set of applications that are used for letting users log in. Downloading and unpacking this package is done by the following two commands:

```
# wget http://www.kernel.org/pub/linux/utils/util-
linux/util-linux-2.12r.tar.gz
# tar xzf util-linux-2.12r.tar.gz
```

Both source code archives are 1-2 MB in size.

Compiling

After you have downloaded and unpacked the files, you are ready to compile the source code.

Compiling Linux PAM is straightforward. The following sequence of commands will compile and install Linux PAM:

```
# cd Linux-PAM-0.99.6.3
# ./configure
# make
```

```
# make install
# cp conf/pam.conf /etc
```

The last command will copy a simple configuration file. Chapter 2 will explain in detail how this configuration file is written.

Turning to the `linux-utils` package, the compilation requires a bit more work. The source code is unpacked in the directory `util-linux-2.12r`. In this directory, you have to edit a file named `MCONFIG`. The file is a long series of configuration options for the utilities. The important option is called `HAVE_PAM`. In order to have the Linux utilities use PAM, set this option to `YES`. The line in the `MCONFIG` file should read:

```
HAVE_PAM=yes
```

Compilation is now done by the following commands:

```
# make
# cd login-utils
# make login
# cp login /usr/bin
```

The `login` program is used to validate the user at the console as he or she tries to log in. The last command above replaces the original version with a PAM-aware version. The next log in will be authenticated by PAM. Slackware stores log messages for authentication in the file `/var/log/secure`, it is possible to check if PAM is being used by reading this file.

The last few line of `/var/log/secure` should be:

```
Dec 10 17:27:10 pamela login: pam_unix(login:session)
session opened for user root by LOGIN(uid=0)
Dec 10 17:27:10 pamela login: ROOT LOGIN ON tty1
```

Extra Modules

Linux PAM is distributed with a large set of modules but you might be in the situation where you wish to use a third-party module. In Chapter 2, an example is presented. This example uses a PAM module called pam_mount. This module is not distributed with Linux PAM or any other PAM implementation.

The module is downloaded from its website (http://pam-mount.sourceforge.net). Once the module is downloaded, it is compiled and installed by the following commands:

```
# tar xjf pam-mount-0.18.tar.bz2
# cd pam_mount-0.18
# ./configure
# make
# make install
```

Fortunately, most modules can be compiled in a similar way using the following commands:

```
# ./configure
# make
# make install
```

PAM Implementations

As mentioned previously, PAM is not a new framework. Today, many operating systems are using PAM for authentication, including Solaris, GNU/Linux, FreeBSD, NetBSD, Mac OS X, AIX 5L, and HP-UX 11. OpenVMS does not implement PAM but uses a similar concept called ACME, and OpenBSD does not use PAM but PAM can be added.

FreeBSD and NetBSD share the code base for PAM. In older versions of FreeBSD, Linux-PAM is used, but in newer versions (5.x and 6.x) OpenPAM is used. According to the design principles of OpenPAM, it tries to take the best from the PAM implementations under Solaris and GNU/Linux. The OpenPAM implementation has a limited number of modules in the default installation but in the port collection (archive of FreeBSD packages) a larger set of PAM modules can be found.

The situation in the Linux world is somewhat more complicated. The Linux-PAM project lives a quiet life and has just reach version 0.99 (April 2006). The major Linux distributions are using PAM, including Novell/SuSE, Red Hat, and Debian/Ubuntu. It seems that Slackware is probably the last pocket of resistance. The table below correlates the version of the distributions and Linux-PAM. As the table indicates the diversity is large. The current versions of Linux-PAM is 0.99.6 and it seems that the Linux distributions do not follow the advancement of Linux-PAM development, as they are using older versions. For example, Ubuntu Linux is a very popular distribution due to its frequent updates to recent version of software. But in the case of PAM, Ubuntu 6.10 (November 2006) is using a version of Linux-PAM released in March 2005. Exceptions are SuSE Linux Enterprise Server 10 and Fedora Core 6, which use recent versions of Linux-PAM.

Distribution	Version	PAM version	Features	Released
SuSE Linux Enterprise Server	8	0.76		July 2002
	9	0.77	Some third-party modules	September 2002
	9 service pack 3	0.77	Some third-party modules	December 2005
	10	0.99.3		January 2006
Red Hat Enterprise Linux	3 update 6	0.75		April 2001
	4	0.77		September 2002
	4 update 4	0.77	Newer build	April 2006
Fedora Core	5	0.78		November 2004
	6	0.99.6.2		November 2006
Debian GNU/Linux	3.1 release 2	0.76	Many third-party modules	July 2002
	4.0	0.79	Many third-party modules	Excepted December 2006

Distribution	Version	PAM version	Features	Released
Ubuntu Linux	5.10	0.76	Many third-party modules	October 2005
	6.06	0.77	Many third-party modules	July 2006
	6.10	0.79	Many third-party modules	November 2006
Arch Linux	0.7.1	0.81		November 2005

Summary

This chapter outlines the problem and the roots of complexity of authentication, and discusses how the framework of Pluggable Authentication Modules (PAM) can provide solutions and reduce the complexity. This chapter also discusses installing Linux PAM: downloading its packages as well as compiling them. A brief introduction about extra PAM modules is provided at the end.

PAM is a concept and a framework. It can be implemented in many different ways, for example, PAM for Solaris, GNU/Linux, and FreeBSD/NetBSD are implemented independently. Even among the GNU/Linux distributions we see differences due to different versions. PAM bridges the UNX operating systems since PAM implementations are very similar. This book may be focused on GNU/Linux, but you should be able to apply the concepts to your favorite UNIX operating system.

2
Theory of Operation

The PAM framework is complex and not very forgiving when it comes to errors. This chapter gives you a detailed view of the working of PAM. The theory of operation is independent of the operating system and PAM implementation.

The complexity of PAM has many roots, and this chapter will introduce many new concepts. General advice would be to read this chapter carefully, and come back to it as you read further in the book. In order to configure PAM successfully, you need to have all the components working together correctly. So you need to understand the complete PAM framework, which is covered by this chapter.

PAM File System Layout

Before we begin our tour into the world of PAM configurations we should take a look at where PAM files are stored.

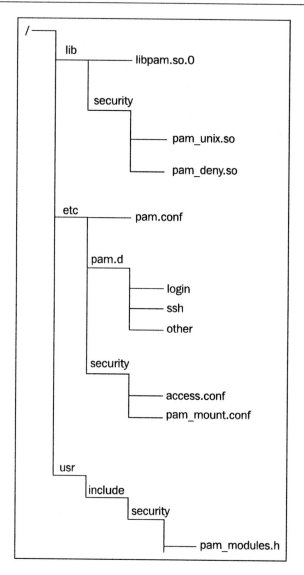

The PAM-aware applications are linked against the PAM library. This library is typically located in the /lib directory with the name libpam-X.so.0 where X is the version number. Typically, it is a symbolic link to the real library, which makes it easier to have more than one version installed. If you're an application developer who wishes to use

PAM in your application, you will find the relevant header file as the file named `pam_modules.h` in the `/usr/include/security` directory.

Any PAM implementation consists of a set of modules. The modules are shared objects (`.so` files), which can be dynamically loaded as the PAM configuration requests them. The shared objects are typically located in `/lib/security` (GNU/Linux), or `/usr/lib` (FreeBSD) and have pam as suffix in their names.

The configuration of PAM can be done in two equivalent ways. You can either put everything in one single file `/etc/pam.conf` or split the configuration by service in the directory `/etc/pam.d`. Most contemporary implementations use the latter because it is easier to work with one service at a time. The Solaris operating system uses the single file model, while Linux-PAM will ignore `/etc/pam.conf` if the `/etc/pam.d` directory exists. PAM-aware applications are located at different places in the file system. The program for controlling login at the console is called `login` and is located as `/bin/login` while other services like secure shell is stored in the directory `/usr/sbin`. Some PAM modules required configuration files beside the PAM configuration to operate. These module-specific configuration files are stored in `/etc/security`.

PAM is not case sensitive when it comes to service and parameter names, while file and directory names follow the rules govern by the file system. This means that you might find examples in lower or upper case depending on the conventions followed by the system administrator. Mostly, lower case is preferred since it tends to be easier to read.

The PAM Framework

As a generic framework, PAM relies on dynamically loaded modules (implemented as shared objects or so-files). A module can provide mechanisms to authenticate users from user information stored in a particular back end, for example, a flat file (like `/etc/passwd`) or a directory server.

A PAM service module is a shared library that provides authentication and other security services to applications such as login, or telnet.

The four types of PAM services are:

- Authentication service modules
- Account management modules
- Session management modules
- Password management modules

PAM modules can implement one or more of these services. The PAM framework implements a well-defined API (Application Programming Interface), and all modules must adhere to this API. Applications communicate with the PAM library through the PAM application programming interface (API).

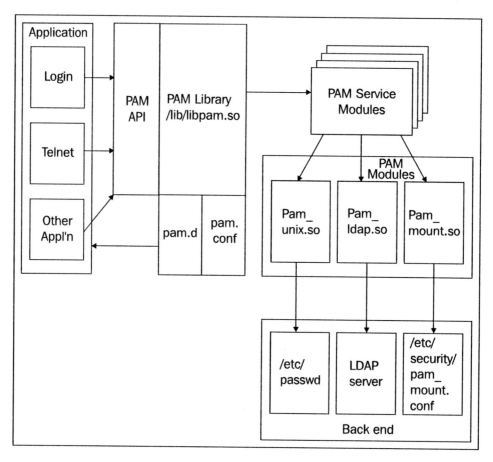

A module can provide methods for authenticating users with a particular back end or setting up the working environment for the users.

Stacks of modules enable you to try more than one validation technique during a single login attempt. You can even require that all modules in a stack must accept the login attempt in order to authenticate the user, or you can choose that one accepting module is sufficient, or mix and match as needed without having to recompile your programs or reboot your computer. This means that changing the back-end user database does not require you to recompile the applications, and you can change it without scheduling downtime for the users.

In the wonderful world of PAM you will find modules for almost anything you can think of. Most UNIX and Linux operating systems only package a limited set of modules. The Linux-PAM website has a large set of links — see http://www.kernel.org/pub/linux/libs/pam/modules.html.

But if your search for functionality is not fruitful, you can implement your own module. Chapter 6 of this book explains how to implement your own modules. Modules are written in the ISO C programming language.

Online Documentation

PAM is documented as a set of man pages. The manual for UNIX and Linux operating systems is often referred to as the man pages since the program man is used to search and display the manual. As always, the utility apropos can search your online documentation. The output of apropos on Ubuntu Linux is shown below:

```
pamela@pamela:~$ apropos pam
pam (7)                    - Pluggable Authentication Modules
                             for Linux
pam_authenticate (3)     - authenticate a user
pam_chauthtok (3)        - updating authentication tokens
pam_end (3) [pam_start]  - activating Linux-PAM
pam_fail_delay (3)       - request a delay on failure
pam_get_item (3)         - item manipulation under PAM
```

```
pam_getenv (8)              - get environment variables from /
                             etc/environment
pam_open/close_session (3) [pam_open_session] -
                             PAM session management
pam_open_session (3)       - PAM session management
pam_set_item (3)           - item manipulation under PAM
pam_setcred (3)            - set the credentials for the user
pam_start (3)              - activating Linux-PAM
pam_strerror (3)           - return a textual description of a
                             Linux-PAM error
pamtester (1)              - test pluggable authentication
                             module (PAM) facility
```

Services

Those applications that require authentication can register at PAM using a service name. The name of the service is determined by the application at the initial call to the PAM library during the authentication process, which is a call to the library function pam_start. It is rare that the name can be set by the user in a configuration file. The Linux box has the following services:

```
pamela@pamela:~$ ls /etc/pam.d/
atd      common-auth          groupadd   other    useradd
charge   common-pammount      groupdel   passwd   userdel
chfn     common-password      groupmod   ppp      usermod
chsh     common-session       login      su
         common-account cron  newusers   sudo
```

Besides the file names beginning with common, each file represents a service, and PAM will use a configuration file named as the service if the /etc/pam.d directory exists. If PAM is configured by the single file, /etc/pam.conf, the service name is written in the configuration file in the first column:

```
login auth    required    pam_unix.so nullok_secure
login auth    optional    pam_mount.so use_first_pass debug
login auth    optional    pam_ssh.so use_first_pass debug
```

In the example above, the service name is `login`. The second and the third columns are management group and control flags respectively. These two concepts are the key concepts of PAM and they will be explained later in this chapter.

As you can see, the services are closely related to specific applications and system administration tools. You can easily guess which application or utility corresponds to which service.

The name of the service is determined by the application itself. The application initializes the PAM runtime by calling the `pam_start` library function in the PAM library. One of the arguments is the service name. Most applications and utilities have the service name hard coded, and it can only be changed by a recompilation. Only vsftpd (very secure ftp daemon) allows the system administrator to change the service name through the configuration file — the `pam_service_name` directive sets the service name.

It is rare to see this flexibility in PAM-aware applications and utilities, but it would be so much nicer to have it. This flexibility could be used by two FTP daemons bound to two different ports with very different configurations on the same computer serving two different customers. Each FTP daemon could use a different service name (for example, ftp1 and ftp2). The two FTP daemons could use two different back ends with user data in order to separate the two customers.

The service name OTHER is reserved. Often it is written in upper case in order to put emphasis on it. If an application requests a service that is not found in the configuration, OTHER is used. In other words, the OTHER service is a sort of default service, and it will typically be configured to deny access to the computer.

Management Groups

Each service can use PAM in four different stages of the authentication process. In PAM, these stages are called management groups. A module provides the functionality for one or more management groups but it might be easier to think about it as a different module for each group.

A complete PAM configuration for one service is listed below. The service is called login and it provides validation of users logging in from the console of the computer. The PAM file is /etc/pam.d/login.

```
# The login service
auth        required       pam_unix.so
auth        optional       pam_mount.so use_first_pass
session     required       pam_unix.so
session     optional       pam_mount.so use_first_pass
account     required       pam_unix.so
password    required       pam_unix.so
```

The figure below helps you understand the service for user validation:

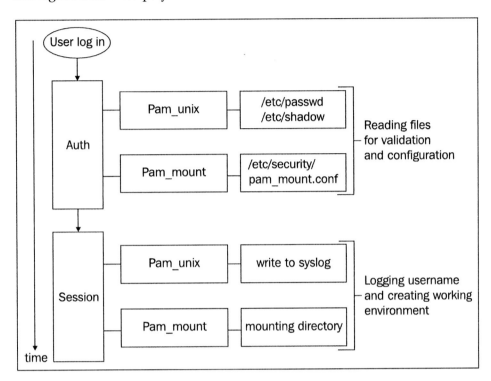

Let us examine each management group one at a time.

The Auth Group

The auth group provides two functions. First, the user can be validated, that is the user provides proof of authenticity. The proof is typically a user name and a matching password.

Second, credentials are granted by the auth management group. The credentials include group membership.

By using PAM, the user validation and group membership are independent of the back-end storage. Traditionally, UNIX systems store user name, passwords, and group memberships in the files /etc/passwd, /etc/shadow, and /etc/group. Of course PAM implementations provide modules, which use these files for storing the data, but it is possible to use other back ends including LDAP and relational databases.

The `login` service example on the previous page has two lines for the auth management group. The pam_unix module validates the user, that is, whether the user exists and the typed password matches the stored password. It is uses the `/etc/passwd` and `/etc/shadow` files to check the password. The second module is the pam_mount module. It is used to mount the user's home directory, which can be encrypted. The encryption key is the same as the user's password, and the `use_first_pass` parameter will reuse the password from the pam_unix module.

Many Linux distributions allow only root to log in on the console. This is often controlled by PAM by using the pam_nologin module by having the following line in the configuration of the login service before any other PAM module:

```
auth          requisite  pam_nologin.so
```

The pam_nologin will block non-root users attempting to log in if the file `/etc/nologin` exists.

The Account Group

The access to a service is controlled by the account management group. You might only be allowed to use a service a number of times per week, in certain periods of the day, or if your account is not yet expired. PAM allows you as system administrator to have fine grained access control – if you wish to do so.

In the above example, the `login` service uses the pam_unix module to do account management. The module will use the information in the file `/etc/shadow` to check whether an account is expired or the password needs to be changed.

The Session Group

The environment for a given service is built up by the session management group, and when you stop using a service, the session group tears down the environment. When creating the environment (or the session), data required for proper operation will be loaded. This includes opening data sources and mounting home directories. The previous example mounted an encrypted partition as home directory. Let me briefly remind you of the configuration:

```
session required pam_unix.so
session optional pam_mount.so
```

In this example, the two modules will write log messages. When the user logs out, the mount module will unmount the home directory since PAM keeps track of the modules involved in the session.

The session group allows you to automate the environment for the users in a dynamical fashion. Many modules exist, and you can build complex environments for your users. In Chapter 4, we look at modules, and Chapter 5 explains how to create different environments for a number of situations.

The Password Group

The last management group is the password group. It is only used when a user wishes to update the password. With PAM you separate passwords changing application (for example the `passwd` utility) from the back-end storage.

The pam_unix module implements the classic behavior of the UNIX operating system, but it is possible to control the quality of the new passwords through options about minimum length. The pam_cracklib module can help system administrators to enforce high quality password.

Stacking

One of the most useful concepts of PAM is the stacking of modules.
For each management group you can define a set or a stack of modules,
which are used in turn. When an application calls the PAM library
function, for example to authenticate, the PAM runtime will call each
authentication function in each module — one at a time like cards from a
stack. The order of calling is determined by the order in the configuration
(service) file. You have to be careful — changing the order in the stack
might have great impact on the functionality.

As example, let us examine the contents of the configuration file for the
XDM service.

```
pamela@pamela:~$ cat /etc/pam.d/xdm
# $Id: xdm.pam 189 2005-06-11 00:04:27Z branden $
auth    required     pam_unix.so nullok_secure
auth    requisite    pam_nologin.so
auth    required     pam_env.so envfile=/etc/default/locale
```

For simplicity, only the auth management group is shown. The stack
consists of three elements or modules (unix, nologin, and env). The
nullok_secure parameter used by the pam_unix module is only
applicable to Debian (and Ubuntu) and can be used to allow login
without passwords on ttys listed in the /etc/security file. The
pam_nologin module can block non-root users if the file /etc/nologin
exists, while the module pam_env sets environment variables for
the user.

Control Flags

The primitive view of the stack discussed in the previous section is that a
module can either return OK/success or not-OK/failure. Some answers
are more important than others, and the control flags can change the flow
and how decisions are made. The control flags are listed in the second
or third column in the configuration file depending on whether the
/etc/pam.d or /etc/pam.conf style of configuration is used.

The following control flags are addressed in the following sections:

- Requisite
- Required
- Sufficient
- Optional

In particular Solaris (version 8 and later) has a much richer set of control flags.

Requisite

The requisite flag is probably the strongest of the flags. If a module is flagged as requisite, and it fails (returns not-OK), PAM will return to the calling application instantly and report the failure.

Required

The return code for a required module is stored. In the case of failure, execution is not stopped but continues to the next module. When the stack of modules has been executed, and at least one required module has failed, PAM will return failure to the calling application. Moreover, the failure is associated with the first failing module.

The required control flag is useful in keeping unauthorized persons out of your computer, particularly since the other modules in the stack are applied as well. This means that a cracker will not know at which module he or she failed leaving him or her with many more possibilities of what went wrong.

Sufficient

A sufficient module can actually be quite strong. The processing of the stack is stopped if a sufficient module returns OK, if no previous required module has failed. If there are required modules after the sufficient modules, these modules are not called. Let's take a look at how the authentication for secure shell against an NT domain (or Active Directory) could look.

```
pamela@pamela: ~$ cat /etc/pam.d/sshd
auth       required          pam_nologin.so
auth       sufficient        pam_winbind.so
auth       required          pam_unix2.so      use_first_pass
```

The existence of an /etc/nologin file implies that only root is allowed to log in. In order to have data for ordinary users stored centrally, it is sufficient to validate using winbind. Validating the administrator user (root) over the network is not a good idea. If the network is not working, you will not be able to log in as root. So if winbind fails (for example due to network failure) to validate a user, the unix2 module (emulating the classic UNIX authentication through the local files /etc/passwd, /etc/shadow, and /etc/group) is called.

Optional

When a module is flagged as optional, a failure does not alter the execution of the stack as in the case of the requisite flag. Moreover, the return code is ignored, and neither failure nor success is taken into account.

Order matters

The order of the modules and the control flags matters. In particular you have to be careful with the order of modules flagged required and requisite, and even sufficient and required.

The PAM modules in the stack are tried one by one. It is very much like executing a series of steps in a procedure. Modules can have side effects like printing information about how they were called or why they failed, or creating/mounting directories. These effects may give crackers information on how to perform better attacks. In other situations order matters simply because the effect of one module is required for the next module to work correctly (such as mounting a home directory prior to reading a SSH key).

A concrete example is the configuration of the login service, which will work as expected: valid users can log in.

```
# /etc/pam.d/login
auth    required pam_unix.so
auth    optional pam_deny.so
```

On the other hand, if the order is changed, which leads to the following change in the configuration, your system will be left in a state where no one can log in.

```
# Wrong /etc/pam.d/login
auth    optional pam_deny.so
auth    required pam_unix.so
```

Consolidating Your PAM Configuration

Most services need to be configured in the same way, that is the authentication of valid users is done in exactly same way, and it is obviously a bad idea to have replicates of the configuration for all services.

Many, but not all, PAM implementations allow you to consolidate the configuration. From version 0.78 of Linux-PAM (released November 2004), it has been possible to use the @include directive. As you might guess, the @include directive can take the contents of another file and include these in the current file. Ubuntu Linux utilizes consolidation of PAM configuration heavily. An example for the ppp service is given below:

```
#%PAM-1.0
# Information for the PPPD process with the 'login'
option.
auth       required         pam_nologin.so
@include common-auth
@include common-account
@include common-session
```

The file `/etc/pam.d/common-auth` contains common or shared configuration for the auth management group, and so forth with the account and session groups.

If your PAM implementation does not support the `@include` directive, it is not too difficult to craft procedures to consolidate the PAM configuration. The short shell script below generates a set of PAM configurations for each service.

```
# !/bin/bash
#
# pam-consolidate.sh
# Generate PAM configurations
#
# (C) Copyright 2006 by
# Kenneth Geisshirt <http://kenneth.geisshirt.dk/>
# Packt Publisher    <http://www.packtpub.com/>
#
PATH=/usr/bin:/bin
mkdir -p pam.d
grep @include * | cut -f2 -d: | sort | uniq | cut -f2 -d"
"| while read file ; do
    egrep -v '^#' $file > pam.d/$file
done
grep @include * | cut -f1 -d: | sort | uniq | while read
file ; do
    egrep -v '^#' $file | sed 's/@include \(.*\)/#include
"pam.d\/\1" /g' | cat -s  | cpp - - | egrep -v '^#' >
pam.d/$file
done
```

It takes the service configuration in the current directory and includes the consolidated configuration files. All the comments in the original PAM files are lost in this process due to the fact that the C preprocessor treats the hash mark # as a special character.

As an example, consider that you have your PAM configuration in the directory /usr/local/conf. The script on the previous page is used as follows. The common files and the login service are from a standard Ubuntu Linux.

```
# cd /usr/local/conf
# ls
common-account  common-auth  common-password  common-
session  login
# pam-consolidate.sh
# cd pam.d
# cat login
auth requisite pam_securetty.so
auth requisite pam_nologin.so
session required pam_env.so readenv=1
session required pam_env.so readenv=1 envfile=/etc/
default/locale
auth required pam_unix.so nullok_secure
auth optional pam_mount.so use_first_pass debug
auth optional pam_group.so
session required pam_limits.so
session optional pam_lastlog.so
session optional pam_motd.so
session optional pam_mail.so standard
account required pam_unix.so
session required pam_unix.so
session optional pam_mount.so debug
password required pam_unix.so nullok obscure min=4 max=8
md5
```

The file login in the directory /usr/local/conf/pam.d can be copied to /etc/pam.d and used as PAM configuration for the login service.

Securing Your Environment

PAM is a powerful framework, and it can be difficult to foresee everything that can go wrong. If PAM is wrongly configured, your environment can easily be compromised by crackers and even script kiddies.

The pam_deny module must be regarded as an essential component in modern PAM configuration. The module can be included as the last module in any stack for every service as a failsafe solution. If no other module has either denied or granted access to the service, it might be nice to know that access is always blocked at the last stage.

Moreover, it is important to keep an eye on the OTHER service. The reason is that if a service is not configured explicitly then PAM falls back to the OTHER service. In other words, the OTHER service can easily become your weakest link — in particular when you do not think about it. A simple version of the OTHER service could involve the pam_deny module, which will stop unauthorized access:

```
auth required pam_deny.so
```

The system administrator is then forced to change (and think about) the PAM configuration for any new service as it is added to the system.

An Example

PAM is a simple solution to the authentication problem but PAM is very powerful, and you can configure PAM to do very complex things during the login process. This section outlines a nontrivial usage of PAM. Don't worry if you cannot understand how the example works — the rest of the book is dedicated to giving you that kind of understanding.

Laptops are owned by people who frequently travel, and they carry their valuable data with them all the time. Losing a laptop (forgetting it in the subway, or if someone steals it) can be very problematic if the user has confidential data on the hard drive. Here, the use of encrypted files, file system, or block devices comes to mind.

Wouldn't it be great if an encrypted file system were to become operational when you log in by giving your user name and password as you normally do? With PAM and a number of Linux utilities, you can do exactly this. The solution presented in this example is partially based on `http://deb.riseup.net/storage/encryption/dmcrypt/`.

First of all, you need an empty partition, which is going to hold your home directory. In this example, we will use the second partition of the first SCSI disk (`/dev/sda2`). Next, you need to install the proper software packages. Under Ubuntu Linux you need to install `libpam-mount`, `cryptsetup`, and `openssl`.

```
# apt-get install libpam-mount cryptsetup openssl
```

If you are running SuSE Linux Enterprise Server, you need to install the packages `pam-mount` and `openssl`. Unfortunately, you must compile `cryptsetup` yourself—it can be downloaded from `http://www.saout.de/tikiwiki/tiki-index.php?page=cryptsetup`.

The encryption scheme needs to be created, and the utility `cryptsetup` is a convenient way to do it.

```
# cryptsetup -c aes -h ripemd160 -s 256 -y create pamela
/dev/sda2
```

The volume name of the partition is `pamela`, and the encryption algorithm is a `256`-bit AES. The passphrase must be the same as the user's password. Now, format the partition with your favorite file system (for example, `mkfs.ext3 /dev/sda2`), and try to mount it (`mount /dev/sda2 /mnt/sda2`). If mount succeeds, then change the owner to the proper user (`chmod -R pamela.pamela /mnt/sda2`), and umount the partition (`umount /mnt/sda2`).

The pam_mount module can mount directories on demand as users log in. The login program is configured to use two PAM modules, pam_unix and pam_mount.

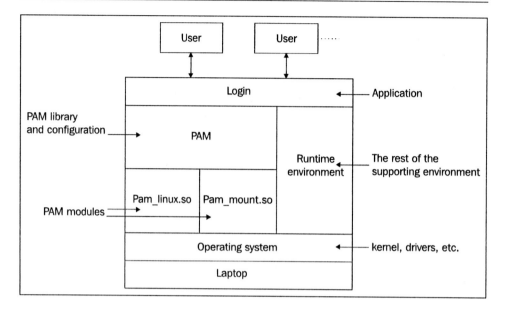

The configuration file resides in /etc/security/pam_mount.conf. The following line must be added to the file:

```
volume pamela crypt - /dev/sda2 /home/
          pamela ciphers=aes - -
```

The PAM configuration must include the pam_mount module, that is, the pam_mount module must be used at log in. The file /etc/pam.d/ common-auth is a common set of configuration related to authentication. The following lines should be added to the file (probably only the second line should be added to the file since the pam_unix module is used already for validating passwords):

```
auth required pam_unix.so nullok_secure
auth optional pam_mount use_first_pass
```

The pam_mount module has the optional control flag. The reason is that not all users have encrypted file systems, and pam_mount will fail. If the control flag was required this will lead to the situation where users with encrypted home directories cannot log in.

The user environment is to some extent controlled by the file /etc/pam. d/common-session, and the file should be as follows:

```
session required pam_unix.so
session optional pam_foreground.so
session optional pam_mount.so
```

The session management group will primarily write log messages and keep track on the number of times the user is currently logged in. The counting is used for deciding whether a log out is the last, so it is safe to unmount the home directory.

Using encrypted file systems with PAM has two disadvantages. First, if the user changes password, he or she will be prompted for two passwords as he or she logs in. Many organizations have strict password policies where users are required to change passwords every month or quarter. Second, if the password is guessable, it will be easy to decrypt the file system.

Summary

PAM configuration is almost a black art for a novice user. The concepts are well-defined but the pieces must fit finely together, or it will not work. The PAM implementations vary but all share the concepts of services, management groups, and control flags. The management groups and control flags discussed in the chapter make a subset of the PAM implementations. Unfortunately, not every PAM implementation can consolidate configuration through the @include directive; but it would not be too hard to generate the actual configuration files by using a set of shell scripts.

The example previously given in this chapter might be slightly geeky one, but it shows you how to solve an interesting problem in an elegant way.

Read this chapter more than once, and come back to be reminded of its meaning.

3

Testing and Debugging

Changing the configuration of PAM is a serious business. Using a module incorrectly might leave your system in a state where you cannot log in and correct the mistake. But the worst scenario is that an unauthorized person can log in to your computer and abuse it. Testing PAM configurations can be challenging. This chapter is about how to test your new PAM configuration so that you are on safe ground; also advice on creating test cases is discussed here. This chapter also shows how the pamtester utility works together with Expect to automate test procedures.

Where to Test?

My very first advice is that you should never try out new PAM configurations on a production system; use either a test computer or a virtual computer (VMware, Xen, etc.). The reason is obvious — if you make any mistakes in the PAM configuration, you might leave a production server in a state where the system administrator cannot log in.

Using VMware or any virtualization system is of great advantage. With VMware Server, a free product, it is possible to take snapshots of the entire computer, which can be used to recover from fatal mistakes. A fatal mistake in this context is that you cannot log in. If you are using a physical computer to test your PAM configuration, you might have to boot it using a live or rescue CD to correct a fatal mistake. And your test computer can be located in a server room far from your office, so correcting a mistake can take much longer than expected.

Of course, the major disadvantage of using VMware is that the host computer has to be able to run VMware and its entire guest operating system. But even a small laptop (with a 1.3 GHz processor and 1 GB memory) can easily be used to test the integration between Linux and Microsoft Active Directory.

Leaving a Back Door Open

It's not general advice but during the test phase of a new PAM configuration you should be able to correct mistakes using an open back door.

In the case of PAM, a back door can be left open in two ways. The first way is to work only on one service (for example, ssh) but enable another log in protocol (for example, telnet). When the first service is working, you can either switch service or disable the backdoor service. The disadvantage of using a backdoor service is that you open a door for unauthorized usage of the computer. In particular, if you use telnet or rsh as backdoor service, you lower the security strength of your computer. During the test phase, an unauthorized user might log in.

Another way to let a door be open is to log in and never log out before you have finished configuring. Once logged in, changes in PAM configuration will not force you out and you will be able to correct mistakes. So you should be careful not to accidentally type *Ctrl-D*.

Which of the two ways is preferred to use depends on the how long the job will take. If it's expected to take an hour or two, simply log in and never log out during the PAM reconfiguration. But if it's expected to take longer (typically it does when a completely new back end is to be used), leave a back door open so that you can shut down his or her work computer and get some sleep.

Test Cases

One of the major disciplines of software engineering is how to do testing. A test suite cannot prove that the software is working due to the limited set of test cases. To prove the correctness of computer software is one of the harder disciplines of theoretical computer science. Instead a test suite is used to find as many errors or bugs as possible. A test case consists of both the user input and the expected outcome.

The behavior of PAM can be very complex. To find a minimum set of test cases can be difficult. For example, in some situations, accounts are required to expire after 60 days of inactivity. Expiration of an account is difficult to test since you are supposed to wait for 60 days. In order to perform such a test case, you can move the clock ahead by 60 days instead of waiting. But such a test case can often be safely ignored since expiration is not configured directly by PAM.

While testing a particular service, three possibilities for each module must be considered:

- Valid user and valid password
- Valid user but invalid password
- Invalid user

In the first case, the expected outcome is that the user is authenticated, while in the two other test cases the expected outcome is an authentication failure.

PAM makes heavy use of stacks of modules where more than one module is used in a sequence to authenticate. Each module in a stack adds new possibilities for how the authentication can be done. A valid user for one module might not be valid for another module. This situation will add further to the possible scenarios and thereby to the number of test cases.

Moreover, additional test cases should be constructed in order to test the interaction within the stack. Interaction is a combination of the location within the stack and the control flag. For example, changing a control flag from required to requisite changes the authentication process dramatically since the module might terminate the process in the case of a negative authentication.

Testing the PAM configuration (encrypted home directories) as in Chapter 2 requires at least five test cases. They are:

- A user with an encrypted home directory (e.g. `pamela` with the correct password)
- The above case but with a mistyped password
- A user without an encrypted home directory (e.g. `root` with the correct password)
- The above case but with a mistyped password
- A non-existent user (e.g. `blah`)

Testing the possible expiration of an account or a password (forcing the user to change it) might be difficult to do due to the fact that you have to wait for a long period of time. Moreover, in the name of completeness, the test of a user with an encrypted home directory where the password and the encryption key differ should be considered. These last cases will probably often be ignored since they do not reveal errors in the PAM configuration.

Getting Backstage

In the phase of testing and debugging, it is often useful to get some information about which modules are called, and what they are doing. Most modules support the `debug` parameter. If the module is configured by a configuration file and not only by parameters in the PAM configuration files, it is highly possible that you can increase the amount of logging in the configuration file.

Enabling Logging

Most modules support the `debug` parameter for enabling print out of debug messages. These messages are written to log files using syslog. An example of two PAM modules with enabled debugging is shown next.

```
auth    required       pam_unix.so nullok_secure debug
auth    optional       pam_mount.so use_first_pass debug
```

The `debug` parameter will enable basic logging, that is you will be able to see when a user tried to log in and which PAM modules were used in order to authenticate him or her.

Many modules can extend the logging. If it is possible, it is typically enabled in a module configuration file and not in the PAM configuration files. In each case, you must refer the module's manual.

The pam_mount module introduced in Chapter 1 has a configuration file (`/etc/security/pam-mount.conf`). The logging is configured in this file by setting the directive `debug` to 1. This is shown by a snippet from the configuration file as given below:

```
debug 1
```

The directive can be set to either the value 0 or 1, where 0 means no debugging information while 1 means printing it. When you enable debug logging for the pam_mount module, a lot of debug information will both be printed on the console and to the log files using syslog

Current Linux and UNIX systems use syslog as a general systems logging facility (a modern implementation called syslog-ng exists but in this context does the same job). Syslog consists of a set of library functions and a daemon. The programmer calls the syslog library functions, which send the log messages to the syslog daemon. The syslog daemon writes the log messages to a file.

Where the PAM logging is directed to is dependent on the actual configuration of the syslog facility. The syslog facility is configured by the file `/etc/syslog.conf`. In the case of Ubuntu/Debian, the logging is directed to the `/var/log/auth.log` file.

You can follow the log files as they are written using the standard tail utility. The `-f` option of the tail utility is for following (keeping a watch on) continuously written files. When syslog writes the log message to a log file, it will also write a time stamp. Moreover, the name of the user who is running the program will be written. In the case of PAM, the user name will be the user who is trying to log in.

Reading the Log

As already mentioned, the pam_mount module will write its log in two places: the console and to syslog. While the console might be useful for the power user, the syslog (which writes to `/var/log/auth.log` in the case of PAM) is probably practical for the system administrator. When the pam_mount module has debugging enabled, the amount of data written to the log files is quite large. A small fraction of the log file is shown below:

```
Aug   5 05:12:46 pamela login[3822]: pam_mount:
         about to start building mount command
Aug   5 05:12:46 pamela login[3822]: pam_mount: command:
         /bin/mount [-t] [crypt] [-ocipher=aes]
         [/dev/sda2] [/home/pamela]
Aug   5 05:12:46 pamela login[3840]: pam_mount:
         setting uid to 0
Aug   5 05:12:46 pamela login[3840]: pam_mount:
         real user/group IDs are 0/1000,
         effective is   0/1000
Aug   5 05:12:46 pamela login[3822]: pam_mount:
         mount errors (should be empty):
Aug   5 05:12:46 pamela login[3822]: pam_mount:
         pam_mount: setting uid to 0
Aug   5 05:12:46 pamela login[3822]: pam_mount:
         pam_mount: real user/group IDs are 0/1000,
         effective is 0/1000
Aug   5 05:12:46 pamela login[3822]: pam_mount:
         waiting for mount
Aug   5 05:12:47 pamela login[3822]: pam_mount:
         clean system authtok (0)
Aug   5 05:12:47 pamela login[3822]: pam_mount:
         command: /usr/sbin/pmvarrun [-u] [pamela]
```

```
         [-d] [-o] [1]
Aug  5 05:12:47 pamela login[3860]: pam_mount:
             setting uid to 0
Aug  5 05:12:47 pamela login[3860]: pam_mount:
             real user/group IDs are 0/1000,
             effective is  0/1000
Aug  5 05:12:47 pamela pmvarrun: pmvarrun:
             creating /var/run/pam_mount
Aug  5 05:12:47 pamela pmvarrun: pmvarrun:
             parsed count value 0
Aug  5 05:12:47 pamela login[3822]: pam_mount:
             pmvarrun says login count is 1
Aug  5 05:12:47 pamela login[3822]: pam_mount:
             done opening session
```

Every log entry contains a time stamp and the user name (pamela in this case). After the user name you find the name of the PAM service, which in this case is login. Actually, it is the name of the program but the PAM service name is always almost identical to the name of the program.

Reading the snippet from the top, you find that the pam_mount module builds up the proper mount command. In the second line you find the mount command with all its parameters. But the mount command must be executed as root (user ID or UID zero) so the following lines show that pam_mount is changing its user ID to zero.

The aux. utility pmvarrrum is called with the user name pamela as one of the options. The utility ensures that if the computer is using SELinux, then a security context for SELinux will be created. SELinux is a security enhanced Linux kernel. Moreover, the utilities find that the user pamela has not mounted the directory yet (parsing count value 0), and the login service will be the first (count is 1). If the user logs in twice, pam_mount should not try to mount the directory the second time. Mounting a file system that is already mounted will generate an error. If pam_mount encounters an error at some point in the process, it will not allow the user to log in. Moreover, if a user is logged in twice, it is important that the user's home directory is not unmounted the first time the user logs out. All this counting should take care of these cases.

We can learn many things from reading log files generated by PAM. If a module can do some kind of extended logging as the pam_mount module can, we can actually get an insight on how the module is working. Working on complex PAM configuration, the log files will give you strong hint on why it is not working.

The pamtester Utility

The pamtester utility is developed by Moriyoshi Koizumi in order to help module developers, but it can also help systems administrators to test new PAM configurations. The utility has not yet been included in any UNIX or Linux distribution. It can be downloaded from its website (http://pamtester.sourceforge.net). It is distributed as a gzip'ed tar file. Compilation and installation is straightforward. The following commands are required to compile and install the pamtester utility:

```
# tar xzf pamtester-0.1.2.tar.gz
# cd pamtester-0.1.2
# ./configure --prefix=/usr/local
# make
# make install
```

Once installed you can start using the utility. It is a pure command-line utility and it takes three parameters. The first parameter is the name of the PAM service, the second one is the user name, and the third is the operation to test. The operation is related to the management groups that were discussed in Chapter 2. The following operations are supported:

- authenticate — the auth management group
- acct_mgmt — the account management group
- open_session — the session management group
- close_session — the session management group
- chauthtok — the password management group

Testing the authentication of the user `pamela` for the login service can be done as follows:

```
pamela@pamela:~$ pamtester login pamela authenticate
Password: XXXXXX
pamtester: successfully authenticated
```

The simple usage of pamtester is to test whether a user can be authenticated. Consider the case where you have installed the Apache module, which takes advantage of PAM in order to validate users for `htaccess` control (Chapter 5 will cover Apache's AuthPAM module). The `htaccess` access control mechanism is used by the Apache web server. When pages are subject to htaccess, web surfers must be authenticated in order to see the restricted pages. This kind of restricted access is often used for hiding the administrative interface of a website. From PAM the Apache server is simply a service called httpd, and the configuration file `/etc/pam.d/httpd` could be as shown below:

```
# For AuthPAM Apache module
auth required pam_unix.so debug
account required pam_unix.so debug
```

At least three test cases must be tried as discussed in the *Test Cases* section. First, a valid user with a invalid password, second valid user with valid password, and finally an unknown (invalid) user.

```
root@pamela:~# pamtester httpd pamela authenticate
Password: XXXXXX
pamtester: Authentication failure
root@pamela:~# pamtester httpd pamela authenticate
Password: XXXXXX
pamtester: successfully authenticated
root@pamela:~# pamtester httpd foobar authenticate
Password: XXXXXX
pamtester: User not known to the underlying
     authentication module
```

The pamtester utility issues ordinary PAM requests and they will therefore end up in the log files. The example above has two cases of authentication failure, which can be found in the log (/var/log/auth.log on Ubuntu).

```
Aug  6 05:11:56 pamela pamtester:
        (pam_unix) authentication failure;
logname=root uid=0 euid=0 tty= ruser= rhost=
        user=pamela
Aug  6 05:12:29 pamela pamtester:
        (pam_unix) check pass; user unknown
Aug  6 05:12:29 pamela pamtester:
        (pam_unix) authentication failure;
logname=root uid=0 euid=0 tty= ruser= rhost=
```

Automating PAM Tests

The authentication procedure is a manual one. The user has to type in a user name and password. If you have a complex PAM configuration with many modules, manually testing it will take some time. Moreover, when you change a minor thing, you have to go though all the test cases again.

The pamtester utility introduced in the previous section is an interactive command-line program—you have to type in the authentication token (password) for each test case.

It is possible to automate PAM testing by combining pamtester with Expect. Expect is a general software package, which can be used to turn interactive command-line programs into non-interactive programs. It is out of the scope for this book to describe Expect in detail but you can learn more at http://expect.nist.gov/. An Expect script for automated testing of the httpd service is shown below:

```
#!/usr/bin/expect -f
# pamtest - automated PAM tests
send_user "Valid user, valid password"
spawn pamtester httpd pamela authenticate
```

```
expect "assword: "send "qwerty"
expect
set timeout 60
send_user "===================="
send_user "Valid user, invalid password"
spawn pamtester httpd pamela authenticate
expect "assword: "send "bar"
expect
set timeout 60
send_user "===================="
send_user "Invalid user"
spawn pamtester httpd foo authenticate
expect "assword: "send "bar"
expect
set timeout 120
send_user "===================="
```

The timeouts in the script are set to fairly high values (1 and 2 minutes; the unit in the script is seconds). The default value is 10 seconds but PAM authentication can easily take much longer, and Expect will kill the pamtester process before authentication finishes.

Bad Example

The usage of systematic testing while working with PAM might be seen as a too serious approach to validating the correctness of the authentication process. In order to demonstrate that systematic testing is important, an example of a wrong PAM configuration will be given in this section. Without systematic testing the error in the PAM configuration might never be found, and it could leave your system in a state where unauthorized persons can log in. The PAM configuration for the login service is supposed to be as the following:

```
auth required pam_unix.so
auth optional pam_nologin.so
```

The goal is that any user except root is not allowed to log in if the file /etc/nologin exists. But setting the control flag to optional for the pam_nologin module is wrong. Setting a control flag as optional will not lead to rejection of a non-root user even if the file /etc/nologin exists. The control flag for pam_nologin should be required in order to make the module work as excepted.

A set of test cases can be defined. They are:

- An existing user with valid password (pamela)
- A existing user with invalid password (pamela)
- The system user (root) with valid password
- The system user (root) with invalid password
- A non-existing user (blah)

Moreover, the first two test cases should be tested in two different situations: when the file /etc/nologin either exists or does not exist. So a systematic test will have seven test cases.

In order to get to the point of the example faster, we begin by examining the case where the file /etc/nologin does exist:

1. The size of the file does not matter—even an empty file can be used. The following commands executed as root, create the file.

```
# cd /etc
# touch /etc/nologin
```

2. The pamtester utility can be applied for testing whether the user pamela can be authenticated. The excepted outcome is that the user is rejected or not authenticated; but now see what happens:

```
root@pamela: ~# pamtester login pamela authenticate
Password: XXXXXX
pamtester: successfully authenticated
```

3. The mistake in the PAM configuration of the login service is realized, and the configuration is changed to the correct one.

    ```
    auth required pam_unix.so
    auth requisite pam_nologin.so
    ```

4. Running the test again has the opposite outcome:

    ```
    root@pamela: ~#: pamtester login pamela authenticate
    Password: XXXXXX
    pamtester: Authentication failure
    ```

This time the outcome is as expected, and if all test cases have the expected outcome, the login service has a higher probability of correctness. Crafting a systematic test will help you to think about how PAM configuration is supposed to work, and performing the test might reveal errors so that you find them before an unauthorized person does.

Summary

This chapter gives you an idea on how to test your new PAM configuration. It is important to think carefully about tests since a wrongly configured PAM may lead to unauthorized access to your computers.

Enabling logging can give you a clue on why your bright ideas do not work. It cannot be said: *The Devil is in the detail.* The pamtester utility can help you generate log messages. Using systematic testing of PAM configuration cannot be underestimated. Using Expect to drive the pamtester utility, it is possible to create automatic testing.

4

Common Modules

PAM is a generic framework, which is implemented on different operating systems. The typical operating systems are similar to UNIX including Linux, FreeBSD, and Solaris. Each implementation varies for each operating system, but a common set of modules can be found in all. Furthermore, many modules are portable, and can easily be installed from source.

A set of basic parameters used by most modules are the same. Moreover, these basic parameters are independent of the operating system. The parameters are typically used to control the amount of debug information and reuse of passwords.

This chapter presents the common parameters and modules of PAM. Using common modules unifies the various UNIX operating systems, and you as system administrator will be more robust against changing UNIX platforms.

Parameters

Many modules support a set of parameters across different PAM implementations. Knowing these parameters and their meaning can help us move between various UNIX platforms and use different modules.

debug

The `debug` parameter is probably the most used parameter, in particular during the implementation and testing phases of a new PAM configuration. The parameter can be used in all four management groups. As the name suggests, using this parameter turns on a debugging mode for the particular module.

Debugging in the context of PAM modules implies writing information to syslog about the progress of the work done by the module.

The syslog facility is the standard log facility on UNIX operating systems. A new implementation named syslog-ng (next generation) exists, and it provides better facilities for storing log messages on a central log server. Syslog-ng is not yet common but Debian and Ubuntu have packages in their repository for syslog-ng. It consists of a set of system calls and a daemon (or service). Typically, it is configured by the file `/etc/syslog.conf`. A logging message has two quantities associated: facility and priority. The facility indicates by which subsystem the logging is done, for example, LOG_AUTH and LOG_AUTHPRIV are primarily used for logging authentication messages and LOG_MAIL is used by mail handling systems software like the SMTP and IMAP daemons. For most PAM implementations, including Linux-PAM, the `authpriv` facility is chosen. Looking at the configuration file of the syslog facility, you will find the `authpriv` configured as the following:

```
auth,authpriv.*                    /var/log/auth.log
```

The log messages for the `authpriv` facility will be written to the log file `/var/log/auth.log`, and the wildcard (*) means that logging is done independently of the chosen priority. The priority can be used to control how much logging data is actually written to the log files. For example, the LOG_ERR marks a message as an error condition, and LOG_INFO marks a message as informational (not an error). The syslog daemon can filter out unimportant log messages by setting the priority. Without this, it could be difficult to get an overview. The PAM system is typically small, and even with every log message written to disk, the amount of logging is small, for example, a moderate busy server will daily generate less than 2 MB authentication log file.

The example below implements policies that are used in programs used for changing passwords. The pam_cracklib module states that the password should be of at least six characters (`minlen=6`) and at least three characters must be changed in the new password (`difok=3`). Moreover, pam_cracklib will check the password against a number of dictionaries in order to eliminate easily guessed passwords. The pam_unix module will store the password in the `/etc/passwd` framework using MD5 hashes for encryption. The module will use the user name (`use_authtok`) in order to select which user to change password for.

```
password required          pam_cracklib.so debug retry=3
                                       minlen=6 difok=3

password required          pam_unix.so debug use_
                                       authtok nullok md5
```

Both modules have the `debug` parameter set. This means that both modules will write messages to syslog. Eventually, the messages are stored in the `/var/log/auth.log` file. The log messages for the command to set the password `pamela` are shown below. The cracklib module complains that the password is too easy to guess (second line) but the password is forced, by confirming it.

```
Sep  3 06:19:56 pamela passwd[4025]:
             (pam_unix) username [pamela] obtained
Sep  3 06:20:00 pamela PAM-Cracklib[4025]:
             bad password: it is based on a dictionary word
Sep  3 06:20:04 pamela passwd[4025]:
             (pam_unix) username [pamela] obtained
Sep  3 06:20:04 pamela passwd[4025]:
             (pam_unix) password changed for pamela
Sep  3 06:20:04 pamela passwd[4025]:
             (pam_unix) Password for pamela was changed
```

use_first_pass

The `use_first_pass` parameter is commonly used in the auth management group. The parameter lets PAM modules reuse the first password entered—from the first module in the stack. If the parameter is not applied in an auth stack, the user will be prompted a number of times—once for each module.

Chapter 2 outlines the usage of a stack of two modules for authentication: pam_unix and pam_mount. The password used by the user for validating identity is also used as encryption token. The example from Chapter 2 is as follows:

```
auth required pam_unix.so nullok_secure
auth optional pam_mount use_first_pass
```

If the use_first_pass parameter is omitted in the second line, the pam_mount module will have to prompt the user for the password again.

There is a common configuration mistake in PAM. During the PAM configuration, the two modules are swapped (this is common during implementation in order to get PAM to work as required). The new PAM configuration is then:

```
auth optional pam_mount use_first_pass
auth required pam_unix.so nullok_secure
```

Clearly, this is a mistake, since no password has been entered prior to the first line. The PAM system and the pam_mount module will also complain loudly as shown below:

```
Ubuntu 6.06.1 LTS pamela tty2
pamela login: pamela
pam_mount: could not get password from PAM system
Password: ****
pam_mount: error trying to retrieve authtok
        from auth code
reenter password: ****
```

If the reused password is incorrect, PAM will not authenticate the user. In other words, the use_first_pass parameter should only be used in situations where the passwords in a stack are identical.

try_first_pass

The `try_first_pass` parameter is a relaxed version of the
`use_first_pass` parameter. While `use_first_pass` leads to
authentication failure if the passwords are not identical, the
`try_first_pass` will give the user a second chance.

If the first password turns out to be incorrect, PAM will prompt the user
for a new password.

The example in Chapter 2 could be formulated as follows:

```
auth required pam_unix.so nullok_secure
auth optional pam_mount try_first_pass
```

The advantage of using this PAM configuration instead of the
configuration presented in Chapter 2 is that it allows the user to change
password. Changing the encryption key is impossible, and if the user
changes password, it will be possible to access the encrypted directories by
entering the encryption key (the old password).

expose_account

In general PAM implementers are very concerned with security—at
least we, the users, hope that. This means that modules will not print
out information about the user since that would make it easier for a
potential attacker.

The system administrator uses the `expose_account` parameter to advise
the PAM framework that the current module can print more sensitive
information about the user. It can include the user's name or login
name—printing this information can make the system appear friendlier to
its users since they can easily figure out what kind of data the system
is requesting.

Modules Related to User Environments

PAM can do much more than authenticating users. It can also build up the user's environment at log-in time. A number of modules have been developed in order to support this functionality. Many of the modules are related to the session management group.

Not all modules mentioned here will be part of the standard PAM distribution but source code is available and modules can be compiled. Chapter 1 discusses installation of extra modules, and fortunately most module developers stick to the "configure; make; make install" style when releasing their modules. This makes it less complicated to install modules.

pam_mkhomedir

The mkhomedir module helps while doing a massive rollout of UNIX accounts. In large installations, centralized authentication is common since the time it takes to create accounts on every server is too large. Centralized authentication schemes include NIS (in the old days) and LDAP. If accounts are not created on each server, the users will lack home directories when they log in the first time. The mkhomedir module creates a home directory if the user does not have one.

A simple example of how to use the mkhomedir module is shown below:

```
session   sufficient      pam_mkhomedir.so    skel=/etc/
                                             skel/ umask=0022
session   required        pam_unix2.so
session   required        pam_limits.so
```

The module can use a skeleton directory for creating default settings (for the shells). Moreover, the default mask for creating files (umask) can be set.

The mkhomedir module is distributed with Linux-PAM and AIX. Moreover, FreeBSD has a port of the module in the port tree. A port for Solaris exists, and the author claims that it is working. The source code is found at `http://mega.ist.utl.pt/~filipe/pam_mkhomedir-sol/`.

pam_mount

In Chapter 2 of this book, the pam_mount module is shown in an example on how to have encrypted home directories. The module can mount a directory as the user logs in.

The supported directory types are not only encrypted file systems but also Novell and Windows shares. Mounting the user's home directory on a Netware or Windows server is the primary focus.

The example with encrypted home directories is:

```
auth required pam_unix.so nullok_secure
auth optional pam_mount use_first_pass
session required pam_unix.so
session optional pam_foreground.so
session optional pam_mount.so
```

Both the auth and session management groups are required. The `nullok_secure` parameter is specific to Debian (and thereby Ubuntu). It is used to control how a password-less account can log in—the tty to log in must be listed in the `/etc/security` file. The parameter `nullok` has a different meaning. When this parameter is used, the user can set the password if it is empty. If a newly created user's password were set to a standard password (say, Welcome2U!), it would be too easily compromised.

The module is packaged with some Linux distributions (Debian and Ubuntu) while it can be found at unofficial repositories for Red Hat and Fedora (see `http://dag.wieers.com/packages/pam_mount/`). If you are using another Linux distribution or OpenBSD, you have to download the source code from `http://pam-mount.sourceforge.net/` and compile the module. Chapter 1 shows how to compile the module for the Linux distribution Slackware.

Modules Used to Restrict Access

When user validation is centralized (NIS, LDAP, etc.), a number of issues emerge. All users are not allowed to log in to all servers, and it is possible to use PAM modules for restricting access to certain computers.

pam_succeed_if

The pam_succeed_if module can be used to restrict access so that only listed groups can log in. The example below will validate user accounts against a Microsoft Domain/Active Directory or local account. If the user is not member of either of the groups with ID 10006 or 10963, the user will not be allowed to log in.

```
account   sufficient    pam_winbind.so
account   required      pam_unix2.so
account   required      pam_succeed_if.so gid=10006,10963
```

The test expressions (gid=... in the example) can test on user name (user), user ID (uid), group ID (gid), shell, and home directory (home). Moreover, expressions do not have to have simple equalities; inequalities are supported as well. For example, you can limit access to your computer so that no system users (user ID greater than 1000 for Debian and Ubuntu) can log in and users must have bash as shell by the following configuration:

```
auth requisite pam_succeed_if.so uid >=
                             1000 shell ~= bash
```

The module is distributed with Linux-PAM, and newer versions support the usage of symbolic names so it is possible to restrict access to the petromod group by the following configuration

```
auth    required   pam_rhosts_auth.so no_rhosts
auth    required   pam_nologin.so
auth    required   pam_succeed_if.so user ingroup petromod
```

If a user, who is a member of the `petromod` group, executes the command `rsh localhost ls`, the log file (the file `/var/log/messages` in the case of SuSE Linux Enterprise 9) will be:

```
Nov  9 23:24:53 srv611 in.rshd[15605]: connect from
127.0.0.1 (127.0.0.1)
Nov  9 23:24:53 srv611 pam_rhosts_auth[15605]: allowed to
pamela@localhost as pamela
Nov  9 23:24:53 srv611 in.rshd[15606]: pamela@localhost
as pamela: cmd='ls'
```

The log file shows you which remote host the user is logging in from (127.0.0.1), which command the user is executing (`ls`).

pam_nologin

Many UNIX operating systems have a policy that only root is allowed to log in if the file `/etc/nologin` exists. This task is delegated to the pam_nologin module in the world of PAM.

The module is often used in default PAM configurations by Linux distributions in order to make it easy for system administrators to reuse their long experience of UNIX systems.

A simple example is shown below (only the auth management group) – the login service is changed so that it includes the nologin module.

```
auth required pam_nologin.so
auth required pam_unix.so
```

If the file `/etc/nologin` does not exist, valid users can log in at the console. But if the file exists (you can create it by the command touch `/etc/nologin`), then only root can log in. The login process will look similar to the following:

```
Ubuntu 6.06 LTS pamela tty1
pamela login: pamela
Login incorrect
```

The user `pamela` is a valid user, but with the `/etc/nologin` present, PAM will simply respond as to an invalid user.

pam_wheel

In the old days, members of the wheel group were the system administrators (or roots). In order to change user ID to root's ID (zero), the **su** utility is used.

The pam_wheel module enforces the old tradition. Used together with the su service it will only allow users who are members of the wheel group to change ID to root's ID. But the pam_wheel module expands the possibilities by having a large number of configuration combinations. For example, it is possible to let members of the wheel group to change ID to root without password by the following PAM configuration line (the parameter trust implies that users in the wheel group are trusted by the system owners).

```
auth        sufficient pam_wheel.so trust
```

But for emulation of the traditional UNIX style, the PAM configuration for the su service must be as follows. A password is then required to become root but it is required to be member of the wheel group first.

```
auth        required    pam_wheel.so
```

pam_access

The pam_access module can be used to obtain the same functionality as the pam_succeed_if module. But the pam_access module is primarily focused on logging in from networked hosts, while the pam_succeed_if module has no hint on where the user is coming from.

The restriction on accepting users is at first configured by the following line in the appropriate service:

```
account   required        pam_access.so debug
                          accessfile=/etc/security/access.conf
```

The actual restriction is then configured in the `/etc/security/`
`access.conf` file. A simple example is shown below. Only users who
are members of the `petromod` group are allowed to log in. A further
restriction is that the user must log in only from computer `pamela`. The
second line is a catch-all line: simply deny access from anything else.

```
+:petromod:pamela
-:ALL:ALL
```

The syntax of the configuration file is similar to tcpwrapper. Three
columns are separated by colons (`:`). The first column is either plus (+) or
minus (-) for allow or deny, respectively. The second column is the name
of a UNIX group, while the third column is used to specify a computer
name. `ALL` is a wild card that matches everything.

pam_deny

The pam_deny module is a very strong module since it will always return
non-OK. This implies that no matter what the user input is, the module
is able to restrict users from obtaining access to the system. As noted in
Chapter 2, the module can be used in the OTHER service at the end of the
auth stack in order to prevent weaknesses due to misconfigurations.

For example you can disable a service by adding the pam_deny module
at the top of a stack.

```
auth required pam_deny.so
auth required pam_unix.so
```

When the module is used in the password management stack, it can
prevent the user from changing his or her password. Locking the
password can in some situations help the system administrator to ensure
that passwords are strong enough if the cracklib module is not used.

When used in the session management stack, the module will not let the
user to start up a session—most commonly a shell. The user can deduce
that his or her account is valid but for some reason he or she is not
allowed to log in to the computer.

Modules Related to Back-End Storage

Login name and password are stored in a proper back-end system, and PAM can take advantage of a number of different systems.

pam_unix

The pam_unix module is one of the most used modules in any PAM installation. The module is used to validate users against the /etc/passwd file in the classic UNIX authentication process, and /etc/shadow in modernized UNIX operating systems. Linux-PAM has a module called pam_unix2, which also uses the /etc/passwd file as back end. Moreover, the pam_unix2 module supports NIS/NIS+ (by the NSS mechanism found in GNU C Library), strong encryption of passwords, and password aging.

Most PAM implementations have shared objects (so-files) for each management group, so you will often find a set of pam_unix modules. Older implementations might have one module supporting all management groups.

The original standard (DCE RFC 86, dated October 1995) mentions the module many times. The default settings for most UNIX operating systems include pam_unix for authentication.

Ubuntu Linux (version 6.06) uses the pam_unix module for authentication, that is, the auth management group. The configuration file (/etc/pam.d/common-auth) is taken directly from a standard installation of Ubuntu.

```
auth     required        pam_unix.so nullok_secure
```

The pam_unix module supports the common parameters debug, use_first_pass, and try_first_pass. Moreover, a large number of parameters are supported depending on the management group.

pam_winbind

Microsoft Domains and Active Directories can be used as back-end storage by using the pam_winbind module. The module is part of the Samba suite, and it compiles easily under various UNIX operating systems.

The application of the module is discussed in Chapter 5. The common parameters discussed previously in this chapter are supported. Moreover, a parameter named require_membership_of can be used to restrict access to a group of users.

An example of the usage of this module is shown below (auth group only) for the ssh service. If the file /etc/nologin is present, only root is allowed to log in. The pam_winbind module is tried first to validate the user. If this does not succeed, pam_unix is tried with the same password. There are two reasons for including pam_unix in the PAM configuration: first, storing system administrators' credentials on a remote directory server is not wise since the directory server can be compromised and thereby all other servers are compromised. Second, in the case of a directory server or the network failure, it will become impossible to log in.

```
auth    required      pam_nologin.so
auth    sufficient     pam_winbind.so
auth    required      pam_unix.so     use_first_pass
```

pam_ldap

Today, LDAP is probably the most widely used distributed user database. Microsoft Active Directory (AD) and Novell eDirectories are both examples of (nearly) LDAP implementations. AD stores a lot of user data but the actual passwords are checked through Kerberos 5. Furthermore, a number of commonly used (pure) LDAP implementations exist, including OpenLDAP.

The pam_ldap module enables PAM to receive user data from an LDAP server. Actually, more than one implementation of the module exists. The Open Source module can be obtained from PADL (http://www.padl.com/OSS/pam_ldap.html) and can be compiled for any UNIX operating system. SUN offers LDAP support in Solaris 9 and later through its LDAP module, and IBM AIX also has an LDAP module installed.

pam_mysql

MySQL is a widely used relational database engine, and due to the dual license of MySQL, it is considered as Open Source Software. The pam_mysql module can be used to authenticate users with credentials stored in a database.

The example below is taken from the *Cyradm HOWTO* documentation (http://www.delouw.ch/linux/Postfix-Cyrus-Web-cyradm-HOWTO/ html/t1.html). The module is highly flexible.

```
    auth sufficient pam_mysql.so user=mail passwd=secret
host=localhost db=mail table=accountuser
usercolumn=username passwdcolumn=password crypt=1
logtable=log logmsgcolumn=msg   loguusercolumn=user
loghostcolumn=host logpidcolumn=pid logtimecolumn=time
    auth sufficient pam_unix_auth.so

    account required pam_mysql.so user=mail passwd=secret
host=localhost db=mail   table=accountuser
usercolumn=username passwdcolumn=password crypt=1
logtable=log   logmsgcolumn=msg loguusercolumn=user
loghostcolumn=host logpidcolumn=pid   logtimecolumn=time
    account   sufficient       pam_unix_acct.so
```

Most parameters supported by the module are related to the database. But the common parameters debug, use_first_pass, and try_first_ pass are all supported with their usual meaning. In the example above, the rest of the parameters are related to the database. The parameters user, secret, and host are related to opening a connection to the MySQL server, while parameters like db, table, usercolumn, passwdcolumn, and crypt are related to validating the credentials of the user. A set of parameters has the prefix log, and they configure where the pam_mysql module will store the log messages in the database.

The pam_mysql module is not distributed as any PAM implementation but it can be compiled from source. Some Linux distributions support it (Debian and Ubuntu as the libpam-mysql package) and it should be possible to compile on most UNIX operating systems. The source code can be downloaded from `http://pam-mysql.sourceforge.net/`.

Summary

Many PAM implementations exist but fortunately they all build on the same set of concepts. PAM became an open standard a decade ago, and the implementations do not vary much; it is possible to find a set of modules that are common to all existing PAM implementations. Moreover, many modules exist as Open Source Software, and they are easily compiled under the various UNIX operating systems.

5
Recipes

The focus of this chapter is practical applications of PAM. Since PAM is a generic framework, it can be used in many different situations.

The number of recipes presented in this chapter is limited, and they should not be read as a cookbook but merely as a set of working solutions. Probably, you will have to adjust a recipe to your environment and your problem. The art of the systems administrator is the art of adjustment. The purpose of the recipes is to show how various PAM modules can work together in real-world situations.

Encrypted Home Directories

The example in Chapter 2 discussed how to get PAM to mount encrypted home directories transparently as you log in. Both Linux and OpenBSD support encrypted home directories, but the configuration is slightly different. The previous chapters have provided the background, and it is time to return to the example in order to understand it.

The authentication configuration can be boiled down to this (the /etc/pam.d/common-auth file in many current Linux distributions):

```
auth required pam_unix.so nullok_secure
auth optional pam_mount use_first_pass
```

The first line does the actual authentication of the user. The classic UNIX style (pam_unix) is chosen, but it is not hard to imagine using another back end, for example, LDAP or NIS. It is required that the user is authenticated, and if the user is either not found or the password is wrong, the login is rejected. In the second line, the password from the first module (pam_unix.so) is reused (the use_first_pass option), and pam_mount uses it as key for the encryption algorithm. If pam_mount fails for some reason, the login is not rejected due to the optional nature of the second line.

The module pam_mount is configured by the /etc/security/pam_ mount.conf file for global settings. If a user has a pam_mount.conf file (or what is configured by the luserconf directive of the /etc/security/ pam_mount.conf file) in his or her home directory, it is possible for the user to control which directories are to be mounted.

Encrypted home directories are not the only supported file system. The original goal of the module was to mount Windows and Netware shares. In both cases, a user name and a password are required in order to access the remote file system. Moreover, it is possible to mount loopback devices. A loopback device is a non-physical device, where an ordinary file in the file system emulates the role of a physical device (or partition). Instead of encrypting the complete home directory, only highly sensitive information is encrypted leaving most files unencrypted. Using loopback devices makes backups much easier since the backup software will see an ordinary file.

Working with Secure Shell

The secure shell (ssh) is regarded as a much better protocol than telnet and rsh for connecting to remote hosts. The Secure shell can be used for logging in, copying files, executing commands, and building VPN solutions. The connection is encrypted from the beginning, and most secure shell implementations are able to detect man-in-the-middle attacks. With contemporary fast computers, the overhead of encrypting the communication is not noticeable except for very large files, and there is no excuse to keep using telnet and ftp. ssh clients exist for Microsoft

Windows so even webmasters can be forced to shift from the insecure ftp solution of the past.

Working with ssh involves creating a pair of encryption keys. The private key is kept at your computer, while the public key can be stored on the remote computer, and you can log in without typing in your password every time. Many hard-working system administrators see this as a big time-saver. But in order to keep your environment secure, the private key must be protected. This is done by encrypting the private key using a passphrase, which only the owner of the key must know.

The generation of a private/public key pair is done by the **ssh-keygen** utility. The example below generates a key pair using the DSA authentication protocol.

```
pamela@pamela:~$ ssh-keygen -t dsa
Generating public/private dsa key pair.
Enter file in which to save the key
            (/home/pamela/.ssh/id_dsa):
Enter passphrase (empty for no passphrase): XXXXX
Enter same passphrase again: XXXXX
Your identification has been saved in
            /home/pamela/.ssh/id_dsa.
Your public key has been saved in
            /home/pamela/.ssh/id_dsa.pub.
The key fingerprint is:
fe:7c:70:dd:f4:48:8c:7a:b4:87:77:76:ee:38:e3:7b
                                pamela@pamela
```

The passphrase (written here as XXXXX) must be the same as the password—otherwise it cannot easily work with PAM. Generally, it is recommended to change a password periodically but for systems in less secure environments, these recommendations might be softened a bit. The public key can be copied to the remote hosts and added to the list of known hosts (the file .ssh/authorized_hosts in the user's home directory) so the user can log in without typing in a password. Some Linux distributions have the ssh-copy-id utility, which can do the job.

```
pamela@pamela:~$ ssh-copy-id -i .ssh/
                    id_dsa.pub alpha.pamela.local
15
pamela@alhpa.pamela.local's password: XXXXXX
```

Now try logging into the machine, with `ssh aplha.pamela.local`, and check in:

```
.ssh/authorized_keys
to make sure we haven't added extra keys that you
                                    weren't expecting.
```

The private key must be decrypted when a connection is going to be made. In order to minimize the time to type in the passphrase, an ssh agent can cache the decrypted private keys. Fortunately, a PAM module exists that will start up the agent with the correct passphrase as the user logs in.

The pam_ssh module can be compiled against Linux-PAM, and Debian and Ubuntu both have the module in their repositories. The installation of the module is straightforward:

```
apt-get install libpam-ssh
```

But the module must be configured manually. A configuration for the login service is shown below. The configuration also supports encrypted home directories as discussed previously.

```
auth       required      pam_unix.so nullok_secure
auth       optional      pam_mount.so use_first_pass
auth       sufficient    pam_ssh.so try_first_pass
session    required      pam_unix.so
session    optional      pam_mount.so debug
session    optional      pam_ssh.so
```

The pam_ssh module makes use of the PAM facility to reuse the password in order to launch the ssh agent transparently. The user obtains a more secure environment and must only remember one password/passphrase.

Apache htaccess Made Smart

The Apache web server supports the use of a `htaccess` file in order to
restrict access to some areas of websites. User names and passwords
are maintained by the **htpasswd** utility, which is part of the main
Apache distribution.

The architecture of Apache is very modular, and there is a module that
can use PAM for authentication purposes instead of standard `htaccess`
files. The major disadvantage is that the module is currently not
maintained but most current Linux distributions and FreeBSD do include
the module.

The module provides the usual `htaccess` authentication, but in addition
it is possible to require membership of a particular group (the `/etc/`
`group` in traditionally UNIX authentication). The Debian/Ubuntu
developers have split the PAM authentication module in two packages.
Installation is straightforward:

```
# sudo apt-get install libapache2-mod-auth-pam
# sudo apt-get install libapache2-mod-sys-group
```

The latter command installs the module for checking group membership.
Using that module it is possible to allow one particular UNIX group access
to a directory. In the snippet below from an Apache configuration file, the
directory `/var/www/` is limited to users who are members of the UNIX
group named `developers`. When a user tries to load a page from that
directory, Apache will prompt for user name and password. If the user
name is valid, the password can be verified, and the user is a member of
the developers group, then the page is loaded. Otherwise, Apache will
reject the request with a message that it could not authorize the user.

```
<Directory /var/www/>
   Options Indexes FollowSynLinks MultiView
   AllowOverride None
   Order allow,deny
   allow from all
   RedirectMatch ^/$ /apache2-default/
```

```
        AuthPAM_Enabled On
        AuthType Basic
        AuthName "PamTest"
        require group developers
    </Directory>
```

If Apache is not running under a privileged user, (which is recommended and common for most Linux distributions), then the Apache user must be added to the shadow group. This is the case with Debian/Ubuntu, and it is necessary to execute the following command:

```
# adduser www_data shadow
```

This might weaken the security of the web server. Furthermore, during an Apache authentication, the user name and password are transmitted in clear text, and it is probably a good idea to use SSL.

Directory Services

In the UNIX world, directory services like NIS and NIS+ have a long history, but both are fairly tight-coupled with UNIX. Integrating Linux in a NIS environment does not require any modification in the PAM configuration, while the Name Service Switch (NSS) in the GNU C Library embraces NIS for authentication purposes, and the pam_unix module can be used.

The Lightweight Directory Access Protocol (LDAP) is on the other hand a generic framework, and a set of protocols and data format, which can be used to capture any information about an organization—including users and computers.

Many vendors have embraced LDAP, but one particular implementation is very popular—Microsoft Active Directory (AD). AD is Microsoft's own version of LDAP and Kerberos. Prior to AD, Microsoft had its proprietary mechanisms for authenticating users. But even Microsoft is approaching integration with Linux/UNIX by using open standards. Of course, Microsoft adds small deviations to the open standards, because otherwise it would too easy to integrate other operating systems.

Winbind

The Samba project offers implementation of various protocols related to Microsoft's products, in particular the Common Internet File System (CIFS). Both server and client side are supported, but in this context only the client side is of interest.

Winbind is a small part of the Samba distribution. It is a small daemon, which mediates authentication requests. Moreover, PAM can use Winbind as back end by using the pam_winbind modules. Samba supports Linux and UNIX, and using Winbind can be a method for integrating any Linux/UNIX computer with Microsoft Active Directory or with a legacy Microsoft Domain Controller.

The integration with AD is divided in three steps. First, Winbind must be configured. Next, the Linux/UNIX computer must join the directory (or the domain), and finally PAM must be configured to use Winbind. The integration will be discussed in detail in the following subsections.

Overview

The integration with AD is not trivial, and many steps can fail. The diagram overleaf shows the flow during a login attempt.

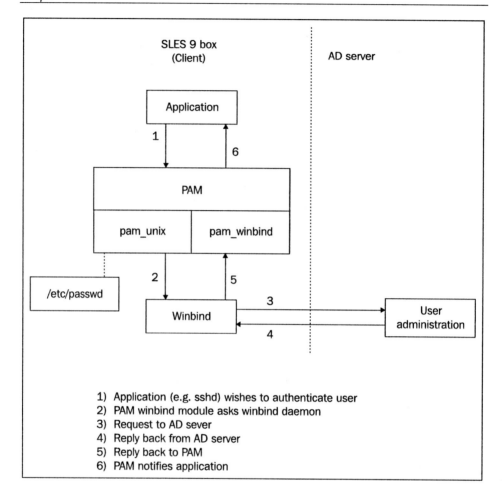

1) Application (e.g. sshd) wishes to authenticate user
2) PAM winbind module asks winbind daemon
3) Request to AD sever
4) Reply back from AD server
5) Reply back to PAM
6) PAM notifies application

Two computers are involved in this scenario: a Linux-(or UNIX)-based client and a Microsoft Windows server. When a user logs in, the user interacts with an application represented as a PAM service. It could be sshd (the secure shell service). Six steps are involved in the authentication process.

1. The application (sshd) wishes to authenticate user.

2. The PAM winbind module asks the winbind daemon.

3. Winbind send a request to the AD server.

4. The AD server replies back.

5. The reply is forwarded to PAM and the winbind module.

6. PAM notifies the application.

Winbind Configuration

The configuration of Winbind is done in the same file as the rest of Samba, which is the smb.conf file. Most commonly, the file is located in the directory /etc/samba, but it may vary. A number of directives related to Winbind can be tuned. The global section of the smb.conf file could look like:

```
[global]
        workgroup = PAMELA
        username map = /etc/samba/smbusers
        auth methods = winbind    # choose winbind
        netbios name = pamela
        unix charset = LOCALE
        realm = pamela.corp        # For Kerberos
                                      (Active Directory)
        server string = pamela-test
        security = ADS              # Use Active Directory
        encrypt passwords = yes
        ldap ssl = no
        template primary group = "Domain Users"
        winbind separator = +      # The rest
                                      is for Winbind
        winbind cache time = 10
        winbind use default domain = yes
        template shell = /bin/bash
        template homedir = /home/%U
        idmap uid = 10000-20000
        idmap gid = 10000-20000
        password server = *
```

```
valid users = domadm
winbind enum users = yes
winbind enum groups = yes
```

But smb.conf is only a minor step. Before starting Winbind and using the above configuration, the Linux/UNIX computer must join the domain. As already mentioned, AD is based on a combination of Kerberos and LDAP. In the sample configuration file above, a number of lines are important to Winbind; the rest are used by Samba for its services. The realm is often set to the domain name when NT dominates the organization. Otherwise, the realm can be used in the TXT record associated with the internal (internet) domain name. A quick lookup using the command host -t TXT pamela.local or similar will give you the realm.

Kerberos

Kerberos is used to log in to the directory, but the login is a single sign-on (this is one of the main features of Kerberos). This is important if the infrastructure consists of more than one server. But in order to get Linux or UNIX to work with AD, Kerberos runtime libraries and clients must be installed. In the case of SLES 9, the Heimdal Kerberos packages work fine. The configuration is stored in the file /etc/krb5.conf. For a simple AD setup with a domain called PAMELA.LOCAL and with an AD server named adtest.pamela.local, the configuration file is shown below:

```
# /etc/krb5.conf
[libdefaults]
        default_realm = PAMELA.LOCAL
        clockskew = 300

[realms]
        PAMELA.LOCAL = {
                kdc = adtest.pamela.local
                admin_server = adtest.pamela.local
                kpasswd_server = adtest.pamela.local
        [logging]
```

```
        default = SYSLOG:NOTICE:DAEMON
        kdc = FILE:/var/log/kdc.log
        kadmind = FILE:/var/log/kadmind.log

[appdefaults]
        pam = {
                ticket_lifetime = 1d
                renew_lifetime = 1d
                forwardable = true
                proxiable = false
                retain_after_close = false
                minimum_uid = 0
                debug = false
        }
}
```

Notice the clockskew directive in the configuration file. A difference of five minutes (300 seconds) is allowed between servers when comparing the time. A check of time is done in order to prevent a replay attack. A replay attack is an attack where a person obtains a Kerberos key and by changing his or her computer's clock back in time, he or she might be able to use an expired Kerberos ticket. It is required that servers that participate in an AD-based environment synchronize time from a central source, for example, by using NTP.

The case sensitivity of Active Directory (and its usage of Kerberos, DNS, and LDAP) is somewhat a mystery—in particular for people coming from UNIX. The first advice when things are not working is to try changing case.

Joining the Directory

The single sign-on to the directory is done by the kinit command. This command will receive a Kerberos ticket, which will be used to identify the client. The command is as follows:

```
kinit Administrator
```

The password of the administrator account at the AD server is required for this operation.

A valid Kerberos ticket can be used to join the directory. With the net command, which is part of Samba (samba-client package on SLES 9), joining the directory is done by a single command:

```
# net ads join -S adtest.pamela.local -U Administrator
```

The computer has now joined the directory (or domain in pre-2000 terminology). It is possible to do some preliminary tests by using the wbinfo command. Two options are nice to know: -u for listing users and -g for listing groups.

```
# wbinfo -u
# wbinfo -g
```

Finally PAM

It might feel like a big detour but finally PAM can be configured to take advantage of Winbind. The PAM module pam_winbind has already been outlined as the solution, but if the C runtime library will use Winbind, the name service switch configuration must be modified slightly so that the passwd and group settings include winbind.

```
# /etc/nsswitch.conf
passwd: winbind compat
group:  winbind compat

hosts:          files dns
networks:       files dns

services:       files
protocols:      files
rpc:            files
ethers:         files
netmasks:       files
```

```
netgroup:        files
publickey:       files

bootparams:      files
automount:       files nis
aliases:         files
```

For example, a complete PAM configuration for ssh is shown below. It is highly recommended that winbind authentication is followed by pam_unix (or pam_unix2) for local accounts. Local accounts include root and it should always be possible to log in as root in situations where the network or the AD server is not available.

```
# /etc/pam.d/sshd
auth       required      pam_nologin.so
auth       sufficient    pam_winbind.so
auth       required      pam_unix2.so      use_first_pass
auth       required      pam_env.so
account    sufficient    pam_winbind.so
account    required      pam_unix2.so
account    required      pam_succeed_if.so
gid=10006,10963
password required      pam_pwcheck.so        nullok
password required      pam_unix2.so      nullok use_
                                          first_pass use_
authtok
session   sufficient    pam_mkhomedir.so      skel=/etc/
skel/
                                               umask=0022
session   required      pam_unix2.so      none # debug or
trace
session   required      pam_limits.so
```

The account section features the pam_succeed_if module. In this example, the module is used to limit the access to users who are members of two groups (10006 and 10963). In large organizations it is probably wise to limit access to servers as precisely as possible.

Turning to the session section, the pam_mkhomedir module is used. The module creates a home directory for each user, first time the user logs in. The pam_mkhomedir module is a trick of the trade when AD authentication is used on servers. Administrators might never log in so why bother to create home directories? But if a home directory does not exist, the user will be left with the root directory (/) as home directory. Having / as home directory can be a serious threat to security and availability since users can either intentionally or unintentionally overwrite or delete important system files.

The main advantage of using Winbind is that your Linux/UNIX computer is regarded as another client in AD. A machine account will be created, and it can be treated equally. The AD administrator will like that. The disadvantage is that the users lose quite a lot of flexibility. They have to use the same shell, and the home directories cannot be picked randomly but must reside relative to a common parent.

LDAP

The lightweight directory access protocol (LDAP) is a widely supported directory standard. Many vendors offer LDAP servers, including Sun Java Directory Server, Novell eDirectory, and Red Hat Directory Server. Even Microsoft Active Directory can be accessed as an LDAP server. In the Open Source community, OpenLDAP is a highly respected LDAP server and client library. The RFC 2307 standard can be read at `http://rfc.net/rfc2307.html`.

It is out of the scope of this book to explain how LDAP operates. Gerald Carter's *LDAP System Administration* (published by O'Reilly & Associates) gives a good and thorough introduction to LDAP. For UNIX and Linux accounts, RFC 2307 specifies a set of schemas that are appropriate to capture the information needed to validate users.

Installation

PAM can use LDAP as back-end storage of user credentials by using the pam_ldap module. Most Linux distributions have a package for this module. Installation of the PAM module for Debian/Ubuntu is done by the following command:

```
apt-get install libpam-ldap
```

For SuSE Enterprise Linux Server, the package is called pam_ldap. For SLES 9 SP3 the package is found on CD 1, and the installation is done by the following command.

```
rpm -i pam_ldap-169-28.4.i586.rpm
```

In both cases, the packages will depend on the OpenLDAP client libraries. You are required to install these libraries as well. For Debian/Ubuntu depending packages will be installed, while the rpm command will not automatically install the required packages.

The LDAP Client

The pam_ldap module is a client, and any LDAP client has to be configured with information about the LDAP server. The LDAP client configuration is a plain text file. A minimal example is shown below.

```
ldap_version 3
host dir.pamela.local
base dc=pamela,dc=local
```

The first line will request the client to use version 3 of the protocol. The second line sets which LDAP server to use, while the third line sets the base name for the directory searches.

The location of the configuration file varies from one Linux distribution to another. Debian uses the file /etc/ldap.conf while SLES used the file /etc/openldap/ldap.conf.

The Name Service Switch

Operating systems like Linux, Solaris, and FreeBSD use a name service switch to control how names (hosts, users, etc.) are looked up. The configuration file is /etc/nsswitch.conf and it must be modified in order to use LDAP. An example of this configuration file is as follows:

```
passwd:        files ldap
group:         files ldap
shadow:        files ldap
hosts:         files dns
networks:      files

protocols:     db files
services:      db files
ethers:        db files
rpc:        db files
netgroup:      nis
```

The first three lines in the configuration file instruct the run-time environment (the C library) to validate password, group credentials, and shadow passwords using the common UNIX files (/etc/passwd, /etc/group and /etc/shadow) and LDAP.

PAM Configuration

With the entire LDAP client configuration in place, you can now configure a service in the PAM framework. The secure shell service (sshd) can be configured in the following way in the /etc/pam.d/sshd file:

```
auth    sufficient    pam_ldap.so
auth    required      pam_unix.so use_first_
                        pass nullok_secure
session required      pam_unix.so
account sufficient    pam_ldap.so
account required      pam_unix.so
```

```
password   sufficient    pam_ldap.so md5
password   required   pam_unix.so nullok obscure min=4
max=8 md5
```

The pam_unix module is included in the configuration so the root and other systems account are not stored in the LDAP server.

Limiting r-Services

The old r-services (rsh, rcp, and rlogin) are considered harmful and should never be used, due to security weaknesses. On the other hand, you cannot just neglect them since legacy applications rely on them. For example, you find legacy engineering applications which use rsh for parallel execution.

You can use PAM to restrict the usage of r-services. First of all, restriction on the r-services can be imposed, but another powerful restriction is to limit the availability of the services to a small group of users.

The basic module for working with the r-services is called pam_rhosts. This module is at least supported by Linux, FreeBSD, and Solaris. It provides the authentication methods found in the original r-services, for example, the use of host.equiv and rhosts files. The /etc/host.equiv file lists which hosts are equivalent to localhost, while a .rhosts file in the user's home directory can allow the user to log in without giving a password.

The pam_rhosts module can disable the use of hosts.equiv and rhosts files by setting the no_hosts_equiv and no_rhosts options. Disabling the rhosts file is highly recommended since knowledge of only a user name can otherwise enable unauthorized log in.

In order to limit the use of r-services, additional modules must be used. In SuSE Linux Enterprise Server 8 the module pam_access can be used. The granularity of the access provided by the module is to the UNIX group level. That is, it is possible to control access by adding or removing users to or from a single group. The PAM configuration is shown overleaf.

```
# PAM configuration for rsh (SLES 8)
auth       required  pam_rhosts_auth.so no_rhosts
auth       required  pam_nologin.so
account    required  pam_access.so accessfile=
                         /etc/security/rsh-access.conf
password   required  pam_unix.so
session    required  pam_unix.so    none # debug or trace
```

The access module is configured by the file set by the `accessfile` option. The access to rsh on this particular host is limited to the `petromod` group, and the user can only log in from either `localhost` or `ux0001`.

```
# /etc/security/rsh-access.conf
# RSH access
# Last modified: 2005-08-11
+:petromod:localhost,ux0001
-:ALL:ALL
```

The reason why localhost is included is that, in the particular situation, the application that requires rsh can run in parallel and spawn extra processes using rsh.

Turning to SuSE Linux Enterprise Server (SLES) 9 the pam_succeed_if module can be used. The pam_access module is supported in SLES 9 but the pam_succeed_if module is much more flexible that pam_access and no configuration file except the PAM configuration file needs to be edited. It is possible to use Boolean expressions, and the PAM configuration is as follows.

```
# PAM configuration for rsh - /etc/pam.d/rsh
auth       required  pam_rhosts_auth.so no_rhosts
auth       required  pam_nologin.so
auth       required  pam_succeed_if.so user
                              ingroup petromod
account    required  pam_unix2.so use_authtok
password   required  pam_unix2.so
session    required  pam_unix2.so    none # debug or trace
```

The `user ingroup petromod` expression can be read easily. In this solution, there is no restriction on, from which host log in is attempted, but the entire configuration is captured in one configuration file.

One important difference between the access and the succeed_if modules is that they are applied at difference stages of the log in process. For the user it does not matter — the effect is the same.

Limiting Resources

If you are running a computer with many users, it might be a good idea to limit the resources for particular users. Resources in this context are the maximum amount of memory to be used, and for how long a program can run.

UNIX and Linux operating systems implement resource limits. The `ulimit` command in the Bash shell shows your resource limits. Moreover, it can change your resource limits (only downwards). The default limits for most Linux computers today are only bound by the physical limitation of the computer. An example on checking the limits is shown below.

```
pamela@pamela:~$ ulimit
core file size          (blocks, -c) 0
data seg size           (kbytes, -d) unlimited
max nice                        (-e) 0
file size               (blocks, -f) unlimited
pending signals                 (-i) 8119
max locked memory       (kbytes, -l) 32
max memory size         (kbytes, -m) unlimited
open files                      (-n) 1024
pipe size            (512 bytes, -p) 8
POSIX message queues      (bytes, -q) 819200
max rt priority                 (-r) 0
stack size              (kbytes, -s) 8192
cpu time               (seconds, -t) unlimited
max user processes              (-u) 8119
```

```
virtual memory              (kbytes, -v) unlimited
file locks                       (-x) unlimited
```

The resource limits can be control by the system-wide shell configuration files (`/etc/bash.bashrc` for Bash, `/etc/csh.cshrc` for csh and tcsh). Using these files the limits are the same for every user. The pam_limits module is able to do a fine-grained limit configuration. Fine-grained in this context means it is possible to control the limits down to a particular user.

The pam_limits module works in the session management group only. A simple PAM configuration for the login service could be as follows.

```
auth required pam_issue.so
auth required pam_unix.so
session required pam_limits.so
```

The resource limits are set in the `/etc/security/limits.conf` file. Setting the size of data segments for each program to 25 MB and the maximal CPU time to 1 hour (60 minutes) is done by the following configuration file.

```
*   hard   data   25000
*   hard   cpu   60
```

Each line of the configuration file represents a resource limit and has four columns. The first column is called the domain. The domain controls to whom the limit applies to. A star (*) means everybody, and groups can be addressed by the group name prefixed with an @ sign (e.g. @chem means users in the chem group). Users are address by their user name. The second column can either be hard, soft, or – (minus). This is how the limit is enforced, where minus means both. The user cannot change a hard limit while it is possible to change a soft limit within certain (kernel-defined) ranges.

The third and fourth columns refer to the resource limit and its value. Many different limits can be set, including core (maximum size of allowed core dumps), data (size of data segments), stack (size of stack), nproc (number of processes), and priority (the UNIX priority set for the user's programs). The default configuration file for the pam_limits module lists all the possible limits.

Summary

This chapter presents a number of short recipes on how to use PAM in the real world. The recipes are neither representative for all PAM uses nor are they optimal solutions. PAM is a set of bricks, which can be put together in endless number of ways.

Using the right modules, it is possible to authenticate Linux and UNIX users against directory services like Microsoft Active Directory. Unfortunately, the success of such a project depend on how AD is configured.

Letting the users in to the computer is one thing but restricting access to certain services and resources is another thing. Again, PAM has a rich set of modules to cope with almost anything you can come up with.

6

Developing with PAM

As seen in the previous chapters, PAM is a very powerful and flexible framework. Of course, applications that require authentication must be aware of PAM. But most basic applications and utilities in the UNIX and Linux world have been migrated. If you are an application programmer and your application requires authentication, you might wish to dig into the possibilities of PAM.

You can find modules for almost any situation, or maybe a combination of modules can solve your problem. But still you might end up in the situation where you cannot find a suitable module. In this chapter, you will learn how to develop your own modules.

PAM-aware Applications

The PAM runtime library has a well-defined API (Application Programming Interface). The PAM API is to a large extent the same on every UNIX and Linux operating system. Only a small number of differences exist, but any programmer can make a portable work-around. The differences are primarily related to the conversation function discussed later in this chapter. Linux-PAM provides one as a library function while other PAM implementations require the programmer to develop a conversation function. The pamtester utility discussed in Chapter 3 provides a conversation function, which might be applicable to other applications.

The example application presented here is very simple. It can store and retrieve data (strings) in a simple (GNU DBM) database. In order to gain access, authentication through the PAM system is required. The idea is that the system administrator can control the access as he or she wishes by configuring PAM in a suitable fashion. This application is called `vault` and the source code is found in the Appendix of this book.

The figure below outlines how a typical application uses PAM for authentication. Most of the usage is straightforward; the application calls a set of well-defined functions, which creates, operates on, and destroys data structures related to PAM. But PAM applies a little trick: the modules can call back to the application in order to retrieve user-related data.

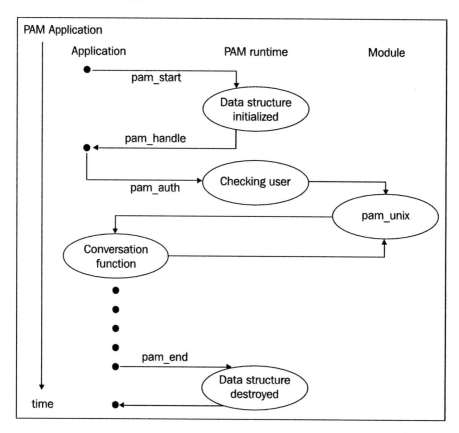

In order to call PAM functions in your applications you must include the pam_appl.h header file. The sample application includes two:

```
#include <security/pam_appl.h>
#include <security/pam_misc.h>
```

The second header file is special to Linux-PAM and it is related to a text-based conversation function and a few other utility functions.

Opening and Closing a PAM Session

Any PAM session begins with creating and initializing a data structure. The data structure (C-type) is called pam_handle_t. During the application run time, it is required to hold one variable of this data structure. It contains all relevant data about the PAM session.

The creation of the data structure is equivalent to opening a PAM session. The data structure is initialized by the function pam_start. Four parameters must be supplied when calling the pam_start function. In the sample application the call to pam_start is:

```
retval = pam_start("vault", user, &conv, &pamh);
```

The first parameter is the service name. It is a simple text string, and if the application programmer permits it, the service name can be set by the user instead of hard-coding the service name in the application. In the sample application the service name is set to vault precisely at the call, and at this point the PAM runtime will try to find the configuration file associated with the service (/etc/pam.d/vault in this example) or the appropriate lines in the /etc/pam.conf file. The second parameter is the user name. The standard C runtime library provides the getlogin function, which returns the user's login name as a text string.

The third parameter is a pointer to the conversation function, which is, the function that takes care of the callbacks from the modules. We will return to the conversation function shortly. The fourth and last parameter is a pointer to the PAM handling data structure (actually, a pointer to a pointer). The call to pam_start returns an integer. If the return value is PAM_SUCCESS, the initializing of the PAM handler was as it should have been. Linux-PAM provides—as defined in the `pam_appl.h` header file—a conversation function, while other PAM implementations require the application programmer to develop conversation functions. Conversation functions are discussed in a later section.

When the application does not need the PAM handling data structure, it can destroy it by calling the `pam_end` function. This is typically just before the application is to stop executing. In the sample application, the call to `pam_end` at the end of the main program is as follows:

```
pam_end(pamh, retval);
```

The argument `retval` is carried along from the last call to the PAM runtime, and depending on the return value of the previous call, PAM might have to shut down a PAM session differently.

Authenticating the User

When an application has initialized the PAM handling data structure, the next step is to authenticate the user. Since the service name and the user name are set by the call to `pam_start`, the authentication can be done by a simple call to the function `pam_authenticate`. The call is typically as simple as:

```
retval = pam_authenticate(pamh, 0);
```

The first parameter is the PAM handling data structure while the second parameter is optional flags. 0 (Zero) means silence authentication but others flags might be valid depending on the PAM implementation.

The return value (stored in the variable `retval` above), is set to PAM_SUCCESS if the user is authenticated. If the user is it not known to PAM, the return value is PAM_UNKNOWN_USER, while a general authentication failure will lead to PAM_AUTH_ERR. In the case of Linux-PAM, the only flag is PAM_DISALLOW_NULL_AUTHTOK which will lead the return value PAM_AUTH_ERR if the user is not known to PAM.

In order to authenticate a user for a particular service, the auth management group cannot be empty, that is the auth stack must have at least one module. If there are no modules the return value will be PAM_AUTHINFO_UNAVAIL.

Account Health Check

It is one thing to authenticate the user, but it is another thing to say whether the user is allowed to use the account. A number of issues influence the health of an account. For example, an account can be expired or the user may not currently be allowed to log in.

The PAM function `pam_acct_mgmt` is used to check the health of the requested account. The simple call to the function is

```
retval = pam_acct_mgmt(pamh, 0);
```

The second parameter can be set to PAM_SILENT, which suppresses any messages from the PAM runtime, or to PAM_DISALLOW_NULL_AUTHTOK in order to require an authentication token. The flag has the same effect as for the `pam_authenticate` function.

Manipulating the PAM Handling Data Structure

In the sample application, the user name is set at the time of the call to the pam_start function, but this might not be always possible, so you need a function to set any piece of data. PAM data should not be accessed directly, so PAM provides methods for storing and retrieving the data items. The function's name is `pam_set_item`.

Many types of items are used by PAM; the table overleaf summarizes the most important types. A complete list can be found in the Linux-PAM documentation and the Open Group's single-sign on service (see `http://www.opengroup.org/pubs/catalog/p702.htm for details`).

PAM item	Meaning
PAM_USER	User name
PAM_SERVICE	Service name
PAM_USER_PROMPT	Text asking for user name

Conversation Functions

The callback feature is also called the PAM conversation as outlined in the figure at the beginning of this chapter. The PAM conversation trick requires the application programmer to implement a function that can handle the call-backs. The conversation function is used by the modules to get the application to prompt the user for authentication-relevant information, for example, the user's password.

The conversation function is implemented by the application and must follow certain calling conventions, for example, which parameters the conversation function must have. The conversation function receives a number of messages from a PAM module, and when the function returns execution to the module, a set of data structures must be set.

But fortunately Linux PAM does implement a generic conversation. The function conv in the header file pam_misc can be used in most applications. The call to pam_start in the sample application as discussed in the section *Opening and Closing a PAM Session* is as follows:

```
retval = pam_start("vault", user, &conv, &pamh);
```

The third parameter is a pointer to the conversation function as implemented by the Linux-PAM library. In order to use this function in your applications you must include the pam_misc header file, by having the include statement at the beginning of the application:

```
#include <security/pam_misc.h>
```

If you are not using Linux-PAM, you might find the conversation function in the pamtester utility (http://pamtester.sourceforce.net) a place to learn how such a function is programmed — see the compat.c file for details.

Working with Error Messages

The PAM library functions return an integer, which indicates how the request went. Mostly, the PAM functions return PAM_SUCCESS but if an error occurs, the `pam_strerror` can be used to generate a text string. From the sample application we have the following call to `pam_strerror` (wrapped in a call to the standard error output printing function).

```
fprintf(stderr, "%s\n", pam_strerror(pamh, retval));
```

Both the return value from the previous call to a PAM function and the PAM handler are used in order to generate the text string. Even the PAM_SUCCESS return code can be used as an error code, but this will lead to text that does to indicate an error (the typical text is Success).

If your application should react to errors more intelligently than just printing out an error message before failing; for example, you could give the user a second chance to correct a wrongly typed password; you must observe the possible error codes for each PAM function—see the section *Return Codes* for a list of the most common ones.

Developing your Own PAM Modules

The dominant programming language of UNIX is C, and it is in many ways easier to develop new modules in C than any other language. It might sound like a huge assignment to develop a PAM module, but many modules are small—ranging from 100 to 1000 lines of code in the C language. Of course, the pam_unix module is typically a very large one. The implementation of the module in Linux-PAM is about 4500 lines of code—a large portion is used to check new passwords.

The PAM run-time environment expects a few things from the modules. In particular the API for a set of functions related to the management groups must be followed. The example module presented in this chapter is a very simple one—about 70 lines of C code. It only operates in the session management group, and it sets up a number of Secure Shell tunnels mapping a TCP port on your local machine to a port on a remote port. You connect to localhost and the network traffic transparently travels to your remote host. Tunnels are often used in order to get through restrictive firewalls, for example, for checking email on your remote IMAP server. The tunnels are defined in a configuration file residing in the user's home directory. An example of a configuration file is:

```
pamela@pamela:~$ cat .pam_tunnels.conf
10031:www.pamela.net:8080
```

The syntax is straightforward. Three configuration parameters are separated by colons (:). The first parameter is the port at the client, the second parameter is the remote host, while the last parameter is the remote port.

The Management Groups

A module can support one or more management groups. Each supported management group is implemented by one or more functions in the module. The general declaration of these functions is:

```
PAM_EXTERN int pam_sm_FUNC(pam_handle_t *pamh, int flags,
int argc, const char **argv)
```

The FUNC is explained in the table below.

FUNC	Management Group	Meaning
authenticate	Auth	Authentication of the user
setcred	Auth	Setting credentials
acct_mgmt	Account	Validating account health
chauthtok	Password	Manipulating passwords
open_session	Session	Open a new session
close_session	Session	Clean up when closing a session

The function operates on a PAM handle (pamh), which is created by the pam_start function. The PAM handle contain all the data about the current PAM session. The argc and argv represent the arguments for the particular function.

A macro (a `#define` construct in the C programming language) must be defined for each management group that the module supports. The macros follow the pattern `PAM_SM_<group>`. In the sample module, only the session management group is supported, and this leads to the macro at the top of the source code:

```
#define PAM_SM_SESSION
```

Return Codes

On behalf of the applications, the PAM runtime calls functions for authentication, opening a session, and so on in modules defined by the stack in the configuration of a particular service. The return codes of functions are indicators of what the function was able to deduce about the user. It is vital for the PAM runtime that the results from the modules in the stack are returned. Otherwise PAM cannot make decisions on whether the user should be allowed to log in or not.

The most obvious return code from any function in a module is PAM_SUCCESS. This return code should be used in the case where everything goes fine. The table below lists a subset of the return codes—a complete list can be gathered from the Linux-PAM documentation.

Return code	Management group	Meaning
PAM_SUCCESS	All	Everything went well
PAM_USER_UNKNOWN	Auth, Account, Password	The authentication token (user name) is not known
PAM_SESSION_ERR	Session	Any error related to opening or closing sessions
PAM_AUTH_ERR	Auth, Account	Authentication failed
PAM_ACCT_EXPIRED	Account	Account has expired

Supporting Functions

The PAM data structures might hold information gathered from one module that can be useful for the following modules. Two important supporting functions are: `pam_get_user` and `pam_strerror`.

The `pam_get_user` function is used to obtain the user name or authentication token. The user name is supplied to PAM by the person logging in. When the function is called, the user name might have been already obtained by PAM in a prior module. Typically the module in the auth stack will request the user to provide a user name.

If the user name is not known to PAM when the `pam_get_user` function is called, PAM will automatically use the conversation function to get it. Whether the conversation function is called or not is decided by PAM and not the module developer.

The sample module calls the function as:

```
if (pam_get_user(pamh, &username, NULL) != PAM_SUCCESS) {
    syslog(LOG_ERR, "cannot determine user name");
    return PAM_USER_UNKNOWN;
}
```

The function returns PAM_SUCCESS if a user name can be obtained. Moreover, the user name is stored in a string pointed to by the variable `username`.

The `pam_strerror` function has already been mentioned. Still, the function might be useful for module developers in order to give unified error messages. Instead of using syslog in the code, a similar code snippet is:

```
if ((pam_error=pam_get_user(pamh, &username, NULL)) !=
PAM_SUCCESS) {
    fprintf(stderr, "%s\n", pam_strerror(pamh, pam_error));
    return pam_error;
}
```

Of course, module developers can use any function that can be called from within a C program. The sample module uses a number of standard C functions for file and string operations. Moreover, the syslog facility is also used.

Compiling

PAM modules are shared objects (so files). A shared object can be loaded on demand, and the PAM subsystem does not require a complete recompile if a module is added, removed, or modified.

Using GNU development tools, it is not difficult to compile modules for Linux-PAM. The sample module is compiled and installed by the following commands:

```
$ gcc -fPIC -c pam_tunnels.c
$ ld -x --shared -o pam_tunnels.so pam_tunnels.o
$ sudo cp pam_tunnels.o /lib/security
```

It is possible to compile the PAM subsystem as one big static system. It might be feasible in embedded systems where flexibility is sacrificed for smaller systems. In such a case, you must supply a structure in the source code so PAM knows which function implements what. In the sample module, the structure is set to:

```
struct pam_module _pam_deny_modstruct = {
    "pam_deny",
    NULL,
    NULL,
    NULL,
    pam_sm_open_session,
    pam_sm_close_session,
    NULL
};
```

This is basically a listing of the functions that can be implemented by a module.

When the new module is compiling without errors, it must be tested. A simple testing method is to set up a test service and use the pamtester utility as described in Chapter 3.

Summary

Developing with PAM might be a new world for you. But if you are used to UNIX programming in C, it is not a completely strange world.

Applications can easily become PAM-aware, and that might give your applications a great deal of flexibility when it comes to authentication. Moreover, in situations where you cannot find a PAM module that satisfies your demands, it is possible to write your own module.

A
Source code

The C programming language is a natural choice when developing either PAM-aware applications or new modules. Chapter 6 shows examples of an application and a module, and in this appendix you find the source code for both examples.

Vault – Secure Database

The vault program is an example of a PAM-aware application. It provides access to a small database where users can store key/value pairs. The database behind vault is the GNU dbm, and it is not a sophisticated usage of it. The program is somewhat dependent on Linux-PAM due to the fact that the program uses the conversation function provided by Linux-PAM.

```
/*
 * vault.c - access to a secure data vault
 *
 * Kenneth Geisshirt <http://kenneth.geisshirt.dk/>
 *
 */

#include <security/pam_appl.h>
#include <security/pam_misc.h>
#include <stdio.h>
#include <unistd.h>
```

```
#include <gdbm.h>
#include <sys/types.h>
#include <sys/stat.h>

static struct pam_conv conv = {
  misc_conv,
  NULL
};


int main(int argc, char *argv[]) {

  pam_handle_t *pamh = NULL;  /** PAM data structure **/
  int retval;
  GDBM_FILE dbh;
  datum key, data;
  int flags;

  char *user = getlogin();

  /** Creating and initializing a PAM session **/
  retval = pam_start("vault", user, &conv, &pamh);
  if (retval == PAM_SUCCESS)
    /** Authenticate user **/
    retval = pam_authenticate(pamh, 0);

  if (retval == PAM_SUCCESS) {
    dbh = gdbm_open("vault.db", 512, GDBM_WRCREAT,
        S_IREAD|S_IWRITE, NULL);

    if (argc == 3) {
      key.dptr = strdup(argv[1]);
      key.dsize = strlen(argv[1])+1;
      data.dptr = strdup(argv[2]);
      data.dsize = strlen(argv[2])+1;
      gdbm_store(dbh, key, data, GDBM_REPLACE);
    } else {
```

```
        key.dptr = strdup(argv[1]);
        key.dsize = strlen(argv[1])+1;
        data = gdbm_fetch(dbh, key);
        printf("%s:%s\n", key.dptr, data.dptr);
      }
    gdbm_close(dbh);
  }

  fprintf(stderr, "%s\n", pam_strerror(pamh, retval));

  /** Destroy the PAM session **/
  pam_end(pamh, retval);
}
```

The ssh_tunnels Module

The example of a small PAM module is the ssh_tunnels module. The module initiates a number of SSH tunnels for the user when he or she logs in. SSH tunnels tend to close when they are not used for a while, and the autossh program wraps the SSH client in order to prevent this (or more precisely—autossh will reconnect). The module use the autossh program instead of the plain SSH client.

```
/* pam_tunnels module */

/*
 * based on the pam_deny module (Linux PAM)
 */


#define PAM_SM_SESSION

#include <security/pam_modules.h>
#include <stdio.h>
#include <stdlib.h>
#include <string.h>
#include <sys/types.h>
```

```c
#include <pwd.h>
#include <syslog.h>

/* --- session management --- */

PAM_EXTERN int
pam_sm_open_session(pam_handle_t *pamh, int flags,
                    int argc, const char **argv)
{

  FILE *conffile;
  char *conffilename;
  const char *username = NULL;
  char *lport, *rport, *host;
  char cmdline[256], line[256];
  struct passwd *pwd = malloc(sizeof(struct passwd));

  if (pam_get_user(pamh, &username, NULL) != PAM_SUCCESS)
{
    syslog(LOG_ERR, "cannot determine user name");
    return PAM_USER_UNKNOWN;
  }
  pwd = getpwnam(username);
  conffilename = calloc(sizeof(char), strlen(
                  pwd->pw_dir)+20);
  sprintf(conffilename, "%s/.pam_tunnels.conf",
                  pwd->pw_dir);
  conffile = fopen(conffilename, "r");
  while ((fscanf(conffile, "%s\n", line)) != EOF) {
    lport = strtok(line, ":");
    host = strtok(NULL, ":");
    rport = strtok(NULL, ":");
    sprintf(cmdline, "autossh -f -N -L %s:%s:%s %s",
lport, host, rport, host);
    system(cmdline);
  }
```

```
  fclose(conffile);
  free(conffilename);
  return PAM_SUCCESS;
}
PAM_EXTERN int
pam_sm_close_session(pam_handle_t *pamh, int flags,
                     int argc, const char **argv)
{
  return PAM_SUCCESS;
}


/* end of module definition */

/* static module data */
#ifdef PAM_STATIC
struct pam_module _pam_deny_modstruct = {
    "pam_deny",
    NULL,
    NULL,
    NULL,
    pam_sm_open_session,
    pam_sm_close_session,
    NULL
};
#endif
```

Index

Thank you for buying
Pluggable Authentication Modules

Packt Open Source Project Royalties

When we sell a book written on an Open Source project, we pay a royalty directly to that project. Therefore by purchasing Pluggable Authentication Modules, Packt will have given some of the money received to the Linux-PAM project.

In the long term, we see ourselves and you—customers and readers of our books—as part of the Open Source ecosystem, providing sustainable revenue for the projects we publish on. Our aim at Packt is to establish publishing royalties as an essential part of the service and support a business model that sustains Open Source.

If you're working with an Open Source project that you would like us to publish on, and subsequently pay royalties to, please get in touch with us.

Writing for Packt

We welcome all inquiries from people who are interested in authoring. Book proposals should be sent to authors@packtpub.com. If your book idea is still at an early stage and you would like to discuss it first before writing a formal book proposal, contact us; one of our commissioning editors will get in touch with you.

We're not just looking for published authors; if you have strong technical skills but no writing experience, our experienced editors can help you develop a writing career, or simply get some additional reward for your expertise.

About Packt Publishing

Packt, pronounced 'packed', published its first book "Mastering phpMyAdmin for Effective MySQL Management" in April 2004 and subsequently continued to specialize in publishing highly focused books on specific technologies and solutions.

Our books and publications share the experiences of your fellow IT professionals in adapting and customizing today's systems, applications, and frameworks. Our solution-based books give you the knowledge and power to customize the software and technologies you're using to get the job done. Packt books are more specific and less general than the IT books you have seen in the past. Our unique business model allows us to bring you more focused information, giving you more of what you need to know, and less of what you don't.

Packt is a modern, yet unique publishing company, which focuses on producing quality, cutting-edge books for communities of developers, administrators, and newbies alike. For more information, please visit our website: www.PacktPub.com.

OpenVPN: Building and Integrating Virtual Private Networks

ISBN: 1-904811-85-X   Paperback: 258 pages

Learn how to build secure VPNs using this powerful Open Source application.

1. Learn how to install, configure, and create tunnels with OpenVPN on Linux, Windows, and MacOSX

2. Use OpenVPN with DHCP, routers, firewall, and HTTP proxy servers

3. Advanced management of security certificates

Openswan: Building and Integrating Virtual Private Networks

ISBN: 1-904811-25-6   Paperback: 350 pages

Learn from the developers of Openswan how to build industry standard, military grade VPNs and connect them with Windows, MacOSX, and other VPN vendors.

1. Learn everything you need to know about Openswan from its core developers

2. Build VPNs that interoperate with Windows, MacOS, and other network vendors

3. Build your own secure hotspots

Please check **www.PacktPub.com** for information on our titles

TrixBox Made Easy

ISBN: 1-904811-93-0   Paperback: 160 pages

A step-by-step guide to installing and running your home and office VoIP system.

1. Plan and configure your own VoIP and telephony systems

2. Setup voicemail, conferencing, and call recording

3. Clear and practical tutorial with case study format

Configuring IPCop Firewalls: Closing Borders with Open Source

ISBN: 1-904811-36-1   Paperback: 154 pages

How to setup, configure and manage your Linux firewall, web proxy, DHCP, DNS, time server, and VPN with this powerful Open Source solution.

1. Learn how to install, configure, and set up IPCop on your Linux servers

2. Use IPCop as a web proxy, DHCP, DNS, time server, and VPN

3. Advanced add-on management

Please check **www.PacktPub.com** for information on our titles

Printed in the United Kingdom
by Lightning Source UK Ltd.
118590UK00001B/75